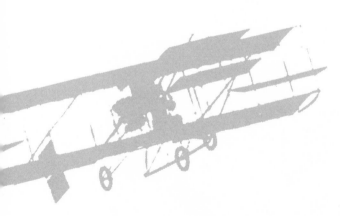

University Press of Florida

Gainesville Tallahassee Tampa Boca Raton Pensacola Orlando Miami Jacksonville

Hugh Robinson

PIONEER AVIATOR

George L. Vergara

Copyright 1995 by the Board of Regents of the State of Florida
Printed in the United States of America on acid-free paper
All rights reserved

00 99 98 97 96 95   6 5 4 3 2 1

Library of Congress Cataloging-in-Publication Data
Vergara, George L., 1941–
Hugh Robinson, pioneer aviator/George L. Vergara.
p. cm.
Includes bibliographical references and index.
ISBN 0-8130-1361-5 (acid-free paper)
1. Robinson, Hugh, 1882–1963. 2. Air pilots—United States—
Biography. I. Title.
TL540.R56V47 1995
629.13'092—dc20   95-10168

The University Press of Florida is the scholarly publishing agency for
the State University System of Florida, comprised of Florida A & M
University, Florida Atlantic University, Florida International
University, Florida State University, University of Central Florida,
University of Florida, University of North Florida, University of South
Florida, and University of West Florida.

University Press of Florida
15 Northwest 15th Street
Gainesville, FL 32611

This book is dedicated to my family, who encouraged me on this long literary road. Special thanks go to my father, Dr. Lautaro Vergara, a published poet; my mother, Maria C. Vergara; and my sisters, Maria and Sylvia, for their support and enthusiasm. To my wife, Kathleen, and my children, George, Tina, and Tessa, for their patience and interest in my book—I give my love and thanks.

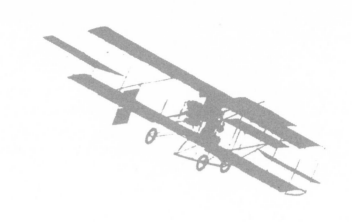

CONTENTS

List of Illustrations, ix

Preface, xiii

Introduction, xv

1 The Early Years: Neosho, Missouri, 1882–1904, 1

2 St. Louis, Missouri, 1904–1910, 5

3 Los Angeles and San Francisco, 1910–1911, 21

4 North Island Camp, Coronado Island, California,
January–April 1911, 32

5 The Curtiss Exhibition Team, 1911, 53

6 Hydroplane and Pusher Exhibition, 1911–1912, 73

7 Hydroplane Flights on the French Riviera, 1912, 95

8 Hammondsport, New York, 1912, 105

9 The Benoist Flying Boat, St. Louis, 1912, 110

10 Aeromarine Plane and Motor Company, Keyport,
New Jersey, 1917–1924, 118

11 Forty More Good Years: Miami to Maryland, 1924–1963, 122

Books for Further Reading, 131

Index, 133

ILLUSTRATIONS

1. Early Bird Aviation historical monument, Governors Island, xvii
2. Robinson in front of his bicycle shop, Neosho, Missouri,
   ca. 1900–1903, 3
3. Thomas Scott Baldwin's dirigible, the California Arrow,
   St. Louis, 1907, 8
4. Robinson and friends with his chicken wire and wood dirigible
   airframe and engine, 8
5. Robinson at the wheel of the Thomas 40 race car, 9
6. Robinson in C. A. Manker's record-breaking riverboat, 10
7. Robinson demonstrating a Thomas 50 automobile, 10
8. Wright airplane catapult, 10
9. Wright airplane being prepared for launch, 10
10. Robinson monoplane, the Flyer, 1909, 16
11. Robinson piloting the Flyer, 17
12. The monoplane at the 1909 St. Louis Exposition, 19
13. Robinson at the controls of Tom Benoist's Curtiss pusher, 20
14. Robinson in a Curtiss pusher, 22
15. View of the grandstand at an aviation meet in San Francisco, 25
16. Eugene Ely landing an airplane on the deck of the
    USS *Pennsylvania*, 28
17. Ely, Robinson, and the Curtiss pusher on the *Pennsylvania*, 28
18. Ely taking off from the *Pennsylvania*, 29

19. View of North Island and San Diego, later site of the San
    Diego Naval Base, 33
20. Robinson among early arrivals at the Curtiss Aviation Camp
    at North Island, 34
21. In front of the "hay barn hangar" at North Island, 34
22. Group at North Island, 35
23. Robinson performing at a North Island air show, 36
24. Robinson at the Coronado Air Show, 37
25. Curtiss hydro prototype, 38
26. Upgrading the hydro, 38
27. Moving the hydro from the shed to the water, 40
28. The hydro on its beer-barrel dolly, 41
29. Preparing the hydro for a test flight, 41
30. The modified hydro, 41
31. Hydro in flight, 41
32. Tractor design experiment, 42
33. Hydro tractor aboard the U.S.S. *Pennsylvania*, 43
34. Triad version of the Curtiss Hydro, 44
35. Curtiss landing the triad landing on the beach at the
    Coronado Hotel, 44
36. Makeshift fort for dive-bombing at the Coronado, 45
37. Robinson and two passengers on a Curtiss pusher, 48
38. Curtiss pusher being crated for transportation, 54
39. The pusher on a railroad car, 54
40. Robinson after a forced landing in Sioux territory, 56
41. Jimmie Ward, 59
42. Stopping the pusher the hard way, 60
43. Robinson and his mechanic, W. J. "Shack" Shackelford,
    starting a Curtiss, 61
44. The Robinson family, 63
45. Robinson among his fans after a successful show, 65
46. Robinson and A. B. Lambert, 66

47. Robinson's pilot's license: number 42, 68
48. Flying under the Illinois Central bridge at Cairo, Ill., 72
49. Air show program, 77
50. Wreckage of the Johnstone plane in Lake Michigan, 81
51. Wreckage of the Rene Simon plane, 82
52. Hydro crash in Astoria, Ore., 83
53. Robinson and Ward in Sedalia, Mo., 87
54. Robinson accepting air mail, 88
55. Robinson in St. Louis, 89
56. The Mississippi River flight, 91
57. Paulhan's first solo flight in a hydro, 98
58. The moment of impact, 101
59. Pulling the wecked hydro from the Mediterranean, 101
60. Preparing the hydro for the First International Hydroaeroplane Meet at Monte Carlo, 102
61. Robinson in the Monte Carlo harbor, 103
62. The Henri Farman biplane, 104
63. Robinson and a female flight student in Hammondsport, N.Y., 106
64. Dr. P. L. Alden and Robinson making the first emergency flight, 107
65. Curtiss flying boat, 109
66. Building a Benoist flying boat, 111
67. Benoist and Robinson in a Benoist flying boat, 111
68. Hull and engine of the flying boat, 112
69. Testing at Creve Coeur, 112
70. The flying boat on the Mississippi River, 113
71. The Lark of Duluth, 114
72. A Cootie model R-13, 114
73. Model 40 Aeromarine flying boat at Keyport, N.J., 120
74. Harold and Hugh Robinson in Keyport, operating the shortwave radio they used to make the first transmission of voice across the Atlantic Ocean, 121
75. Billboard outside Keyport, 121

76. The Opa-Locka town hall,   123

77. Robinson and the rest of the Opa-Locka town council,   124

78. The fifth wheel on the Aerocar,   125

79. The Aerocar plant in Opa-Locka,   126

80. An Aerocar near the Opa-Locka town hall,   127

81. Robinson at a Miami Air Show,   129

82. Robinson at National Scientific Laboratories
    in Washington, D.C.,   130

For centuries humans dreamed of flying, but not until the modern age of discovery and invention did those dreams become practical. Scientific knowledge turned flights of fantasy into real flight. But there were no multibillion-dollar government research grants producing computer models or feasibility studies. The earliest aircraft were built from crude designs sketched on the walls of the workshops. Pilots learned to fly by wedging themselves into their flimsy planes made of bamboo, linen, and bailing wire—and flying.

The early aviators tested their ideas themselves, with little textbook understanding of aerodynamics. To finance their work they performed exhibitions in which accidents were seemingly inevitable; many died making the dream of flight a reality.

One pioneer aviator, Hugh Robinson Sr., survived the test flights and the air shows and helped make flying an integral part of the business of life. Nearly as meticulous a historian as he was an engineer, he maintained a fascinating file of memorabilia, which I used to write and illustrate this book. I wrote to honor Hugh's memory and the memory of all the early fliers, who continue to inspire us to make our dreams come true.

I am grateful to Arva Parks, one of Florida's premier historians, who encouraged me to complete this project. Many thanks are due also to Paul Garber of the Smithsonian Aerospace Museum for his encouragement; to the staff of the Curtiss Museum in Hammondsport, New York; to the San

Diego Aerospace Museum; to the St. Petersburg Historical Society; and to the Florida Aviation Historical Society, Flight One Museum, St. Petersburg. I am indebted to John C. Nordt III, M.D., and his father, John Nordt II, for flying me to many parts of the country to gather information.

My gratitude goes to my sister, Maria Vergara-Wilson, and my wife, Kathleen C. Vergara, for their valuable contributions to this project, and to Ann Boyd, who was most helpful in organizing the material.

I am greatly indebted to Jack Stark—author, aviation editor of the *Miami Herald,* and personal friend of Hugh Robinson—who assisted me in the preliminary editing of the manuscript.

Finally, special thanks go to Janet Herron and Joan Miller for their help in the final editing and to Owen Billman, Thomas O'Brian, and Stella Ferrer for reading the manuscript and offering their encouragement.

Hugh Robinson Jr. had been my patient for several years, and through this association we developed a friendship. He was a modest, quiet man who had never revealed to me that his father was one of the pioneers of aviation.

One day as we conferred in my office, he shyly asked me if I would be interested in seeing some of his father's scrapbooks. He told me that his father had been one of the first people to fly an airplane. I jumped at the invitation. A few days later Hugh brought me a large and battered cardboard box. Inside were a dozen scrapbooks filled with pictures of early flying machines and hundreds of carefully preserved newspaper clippings about his father's contributions to aeronautics. That evening I spent hours poring over the photographs. None were labeled, and there were few that I recognized or could appreciate. But the experience was intriguing, and I felt privileged to have the opportunity to share in Hugh's pride in his father.

The next day I returned the box, expressing to Hugh my thanks for his generosity and my enthusiasm over his treasure. To my surprise, he refused to accept the box and asked me to review the contents once more. He felt that I had not appreciated the historical value of the material.

Puzzled, I reopened the box. A small pamphlet caught my eye. In it was a picture of a plaque mounted on a monument at Governor's Island,

New York, dedicated to the aviation pioneers who had flown there between 1909 and 1916. First on the list of fifteen names were Wilbur Wright and Glenn Curtiss—names familiar to everyone. Other names, such as Lincoln Beachy and Eugene Ely, would be familiar to students of aviation history. I was astonished to see the name of Hugh Robinson on that plaque (fig. 1). Suddenly I realized the significance of the photographs and clippings. Hugh Robinson was not merely a random flier. He was an important early American aviator, and what he saved in that box could give me a view of the lives of the early fliers that I could get nowhere else.

I resolved to organize the treasure trove I had acquired. In the beginning I did it to satisfy my curiosity as a former pilot, though I also wished to honor my gracious and generous friend. As I became more involved in the work I grew increasingly astonished that so much of early aviation history lay in my hands. To organize the material took me several years and required a great deal of research. Hugh Robinson Jr. worked closely with me, and we shared many hours reconstructing his father's adventures.

During this period of discovery, Hugh's health failed, and he passed away. I grieved the loss of a close friend and determined to put the material together as a tribute, both to the father and the son. The family of Hugh Robinson Jr.—his wife, Willie, his grandchildren, and his brother, Harold—assisted me in interpreting the material and gathering more information. Eventually my research led me to the National Air and Space Museum of the Smithsonian Institution, where I shared my explorations with Paul Garber, one of the museum's founders and its director emeritus. An acquaintance of Hugh Sr., he encouraged me to continue.

Together we marveled over the Robinson family's careful preservation of the material. Few of the other pioneer pilots had saved their photographs or newspaper clippings. Thus the collection provided a rare glimpse at a magnificent era of discovery, daring, and innovation. I began to give slide lectures on Hugh Robinson to pilot groups, but it was not long be-

1. *The Early Bird Aviation Historical Monument on Governors Island in New York commemorates the pioneers who made historic flights there from 1909 to 1916. Wilbur Wright made the first flight around the Statue of Liberty on May 29, 1910. Glenn Curtiss landed on the island to complete his historic flight from Albany to New York City on May 29, 1910, for which he won $10,000.00. Hugh Robinson, Lincoln Beachy, and Eugene Ely started their race from Governors Island to Philadelphia on August 5, 1911, competing for a prize of $5,000.00.*

fore I realized that the Robinson story should be made available to a wider audience.

The story of Glenn Curtiss's contributions to aviation has been well documented over the years. He was certainly a genius, but he completed only an elementary-school education. His success therefore depended in part upon the talented men who surrounded him. Hugh Robinson, a college-educated engineer, was one of those men.

This book documents the flowering of aviation through the life of Hugh Robinson. Much of the information here is based on the clippings and photos Hugh Jr. shared with me. Most of them were not strictly identified. Many of the photos were taken by Glenn Curtiss's photographer and meticulously saved by Robinson. Other photos were taken by Robinson himself or by unidentified photographers.

CHAPTER 1

The Early Years:
Neosho, Missouri, 1882–1904

He stood at the top of the steps on Neosho's Big Springs Hill, looking down at the bottom, more than a hundred feet below. His white knuckles gripped the handlebars of his homemade bicycle, built in his father's lumbermill and built for strength. He studied the group of Neosho youths who were taunting him to push off. His eyes bore the cold determination of a born daredevil. He had been challenged to do it, so he did it.

The wind chipped at his skinny, stockinged legs, and his thin face was set in firm lines. His body jarred over the hundred steps that led to a horizontal observation landing halfway down. He bumped and then picked up speed, hit the landing, and flew off the steps into the air before falling in a heap on the ground. The bike was demolished. But Hugh Robinson had leapt into aerial history—on a bicycle that now lay in ruins at the bottom of Big Springs Hill.

Despite his parents' horror over his joyride, Hugh was determined to try again. He built another bike, and this time added a small motor. A Neosho resident named Bell, quoted in a Joplin, Missouri, newspaper article, said that "Hugh made the first motorcycle that ever shrieked its blinding way into Neosho!" Hugh rode through town at speeds of 60 miles an hour for several days, but then the bulky contraption threw him head over heels. A Neosho doctor painstakingly picked the pieces of gravel from his back.

On May 13, 1882, a quiet spring day, Hugh Armstrong Robinson was born to James and Missouri Robinson in the small town of Neosho, Missouri. Hugh was an unobtrusive youngster who spent much of his time reading science fiction stories and figuring out how to make gadgets that would either fly, spin, spiral, or take off from an imaginary landing strip. In the 1890s the bicycle was the most popular and liberating vehicle available, and bicycles and bicycle repair shops were in every city and town. When most of the neighborhood children were outside playing games, Hugh was building bikes and other mechanized contraptions. When his friends came to his house, they didn't play games; instead Hugh would perform stunts for them. Soon he had these youngsters jumping off the barn, using umbrellas for parachutes. By the age of fourteen, Hugh had jumped out of a hot-air balloon in a parachute in front of the entire community.

In an attempt to bring some order to Hugh's life—and to prolong it—his parents insisted that he go to college. He entered Webb City Baptist College in Carthage, Missouri, in 1898 and earned a mechanical engineering degree in 1900.

Hugh's parents were prominent townspeople who owned a lumber mill and hardware business. Recognizing Hugh's mechanical talents, his parents set him up in his own repair shop, which he operated from 1900 to 1903. A sign in the front window read, "WE REPAIR ANYTHING" (fig. 2). Nothing daunted Hugh, and he learned to fix all kinds of broken appliances and machines.

Hugh was now in his element, and before long he designed and built an automobile in the back of the repair shop. It was neon red, fashioned in the buckboard style, and he named it the Red Devil. He outfitted it with a mail-order engine and bicycle wheels. Soon the Red Devil flew its maiden flight down Neosho's streets in a cloud of dust, much to the chagrin of the townspeople—and the town animals. The local newspaper observed, "Ev-

2. Robinson in the doorway of his Neosho, Missouri, bicycle shop, which he operated from 1900 to 1903 after graduating from college with a degree in mechanical engineering. The automobile he constructed—the Red Devil—is parked in front. Note the sign in the window that reads, "WE REPAIR ANYTHING." In 1904 Robinson and his family moved to St. Louis, where Robinson took a job as foreman of the repair and machine shop for the Dorris Automobile Company.

ery mule in the Neosho township developed nervous prostration while placid cows contracted hysteria and well behaved ducks became flighty and eccentric."

Neosho divided into two factions upon the appearance of the Red Devil. One faction contended that Hugh would be killed in a week. The other held that he couldn't possibly survive another day in the ridiculous contraption. Neither prediction came true, but Neosho's first automobile soon came to a fearsome end. Again doctors had to remove the gravel and grit from Hugh's hide.

Robinson had a flair for circus performance. In 1902 he invented his own act, the Circle of Death, so named for the latticed steel globe that could be rotated while he went around and around inside it on a bicycle. Since many of his performances took place on small stages or cramped areas at the circus, he was compelled to invent an "arresting gear" to stop the bicycle.

By this time certain of Hugh's personality traits were apparent: not only was he a compulsive inventor and a risk-taker; he was also a showman for pay.

C H A P T E R   2

St. Louis, Missouri, 1904–1910

In 1901 Robinson married Estia Emma Heneks of Neosho, Missouri, and within a few years the couple had two sons: Hugh Jr. and Harold. Robinson's desire for a more stable income and his boredom with the bicycle shop prompted him to search for new employment. In 1904 the young family moved from their hometown to St. Louis, where Robinson was hired by the Dorris Automobile Company as foreman of the repair and machine shop. In that opportune environment he found the resources to continue his efforts to create a flying machine.

The 1904 St. Louis Louisiana Purchase Exposition had just opened, and Robinson found additional work as an electrician. It was at the Exposition, more commonly known as the St. Louis World's Fair, that he met and mingled with the country's foremost balloon pilots. Robinson was impressed by the sustained flight of Captain Thomas Scott Baldwin's dirigible, the California Arrow, piloted by famed balloonist Roy Knabenshue. Robinson and Baldwin met at the St. Louis Exposition amid the whir of small engines, balloons, and dirigibles.

It is important to remember that at this time there were no airplanes known to Hugh Robinson or the general public. In 1903 Professor Samuel Pierpont Langley, a highly respected and internationally known scientist, with combined resources from the Smithsonian Institution in Washington, D.C., and other government agencies, built and tested a highly publicized heavier-than-air machine. His craft, called the Great Aerodrome, had a movable multiposition tail to enable it to gain or lose altitude. It also had a moving rudder to control direction and a unique water-cooled internal-combustion engine. At full throttle this aircraft produced fifty-two units of horsepower.

The test flight, conducted in Washington, D.C., was a disaster. One of the plane's main structural cables caught on the launching catapult used to project the aircraft into the air and irreparably damaged the plane. The Great Aerodrome crumpled like a fan and fell into the Potomac as Washingtonians watched in horror. Fliers had yet to earn their wings, and this event convinced the public, the press, and the government that humans were not destined to fly.

Two months later, with minimal financial backing and primitive facilities, Orville and Wilbur Wright quietly accomplished the magnificent feat of a controlled flight. At the isolated beachfront at Kitty Hawk, North Carolina, in December 1903, the Wrights lifted their newly constructed biplane into the air. They flew for twelve seconds along a level course without reduction of speed and landed safely. The Wright brothers had discovered the secret of controlled flight by warping the wings to function as ailerons, which gave the aircraft lateral stability.

Only five people had observed this historic moment. The concept was so simple that the Wrights feared their discovery would be copied, so they quietly applied for a patent. After Professor Langley's failure in Washington, the U.S. government showed little interest in the practicality of airplanes. By contrast, European interest in aviation had burgeoned, and government contracts there had become a possibility. At an exhibition in France, Wilbur Wright flew for three minutes, forty-one seconds, and the spectators went wild. Soon after this demonstration, an aviation firm guaranteed the Wright brothers a contract for the sole right to manufacture the craft. It was required, however, that the Wrights carry two persons aloft as well as enough fuel for 120 miles. A LeMans clipping dated September 1908 stated, "Mr. Wright went four times 'round the racecourse at an average height of 70 feet, now rising, then falling at will, and executing the most complicated turnings, figures of eight and serpentine movements. He came down like a butterfly."

Meanwhile, back in St. Louis, Robinson's passion for aviation persisted. In 1904 he designed and built a glider. His plan was to have a friend pull the glider by a rope with his automobile in an attempt to get the glider off the ground and keep it airborne. The maiden flight took place on a gravel road on the campus of Washington University. On the morning of the flight, the glider was assembled and tied to the bumper of his friend's car. The glider lifted into the air, but a cloud of dust obscured the driver's vision, and it was impossible for him to see how high Robinson was flying when they reached an exit gate near the end of the road. Apparently Robinson was not high enough; both wings were sheared off the glider, and the craft was destroyed. Robinson survived the mishap with only cuts and bruises.

In 1907 the competition for the Gordon Bennett Balloon Trophy was held in St. Louis. Balloons and dirigibles were brought from around the world to participate. Lincoln Beachy, who won the race and was unknown to Robinson at the time, was to become his aviation student three years later. Cromwell Dixon, who at age fourteen was the world's youngest balloon aeronaut, flew his Sky Bicycle in the race. Five years later Dixon and Robinson would participate in an airplane flying exhibition in Kansas. The most famous balloonist of all was Captain Baldwin, whose California Arrow, flown by Roy Knabenshue, won third prize (fig. 3). Robinson again saw Baldwin at this race, and it was Baldwin who inspired Robinson to become involved in ballooning.

Robinson was entranced by the aerial display, and soon afterward he built a dirigible with an engine of his own design on the airframe (fig. 4). The apparatus was hauled by wagon to East St. Louis for its first flight. The dirigible was inflated with hydrogen generated on the field by putting scrap iron cuttings into sulfuric acid.

It was to be launched from the Schwartz farm at Horseshoe Lake and to

3. Thomas Scott Baldwin's California Arrow at the Gordon Bennett Balloon Trophy competition, St. Louis, 1907. Baldwin inspired Robinson to take up ballooning.

4. Robinson, fourth from right, showing off his chicken wire and wood dirigible airframe and engine, which he built soon after the St. Louis balloon competition. The forty-horsepower engine Robinson installed was not powerful enough to control the dirigible, and on its first flight it knocked down power lines in East St. Louis. Equipped with a more powerful engine, the dirigible later made many successful flights.

land at Edgemont, Illinois. A storm appeared, however, and the dirigible's flight was postponed until the following day. Reinflating the bag with hydrogen took longer than anticipated, and it was late afternoon by the time Robinson got his aircraft aloft. The air was calm, and the forty-horsepower engine was not powerful enough for controlled flight. Robinson drifted about the countryside knocking down power lines, putting much of East St. Louis in the dark.

The helpless dirigible drifted for five miles before coming to rest on top of a tree near the lake where the flight had originated. Robinson remained with the aircraft until the next day, when he was rescued by boat. He was able to salvage the engine, and after making some changes, he rebuilt the badly damaged dirigible and later flew it on many successful flights.

By 1908 Robinson had become the leading engine mechanic and designer in St. Louis. He patented a two-cycle engine that had taken him five years to develop. During this period he was frequently seen at the racetrack, either racing himself or helping other drivers improve engine performance and speed (fig. 5). Because of his expertise in engine design and operation, Robinson was asked to be the engineer of the boat that set a new world record for riverboating, racing at forty-five miles per hour on the Missouri River in St. Louis (fig. 6). In 1906 Robinson had begun to demonstrate the Thomas 50 Automobile (fig. 7). In those days few people knew how to drive and maintain an automobile, much less such a powerful model as the Thomas 50.

5. Robinson test-driving the Thomas 40 race car to make sure the engine was prepared for maximum stress, St. Louis, 1907. The Thomas 40 won a ten-mile race on July 4 that year.

6. Robinson operating the engine at the rear of C. A. Manker's speedboat, which broke the world speed record for riverboating in 1907.

7. Robinson demonstrating a Thomas 50 in Forest Park, St. Louis. Driving and maintaining automobiles was a new art, and powerful cars such as this one demanded experience.

8. These men were not drilling for oil. They were pulling up a weight that, when dropped, catapulted an early Wright airplane into the air. This method was devised to help the low-powered planes take off.

9. The catapult rope being attached to the front of the Wright airplane in preparation for launch.

In 1908 Robinson met the businessman L. D. Schoenberg, who asked Robinson to chauffeur him on a seven-thousand-mile motor trip across Europe. Anxious to learn of advances in aviation on the Continent, Robinson enthusiastically accepted the offer. While in France, he witnessed Wilbur Wright performing one of his early flights (figs. 8 and 9) and was able to observe firsthand the innovative methods the Wright brothers used to stabilize and control their airplane in flight.

Upon his return to the States, Robinson summarized the state of the art of aviation in Europe in the following article, written in 1909 for *Auto Review:*

Aeronautics in Europe

Impressions of Possibilities in Air Navigation
Gained Across the Water.

BALLOONS AND DIRIGIBLES

The average person does not realize how closely the automobile is associated with the air craft of the present day. It is a fact that the construction of the mechanical plant of dirigibles and aeroplanes is practically the same as that used in automobiles. Aeronautical motors are necessarily more lightly built than those of the auto but the material construction is the same.

In the United States the public does not see or read so much of aeronautics as in Europe, owing to the fact that Europe is several years ahead of us in this particular line of development. In France it has reached a point where it is being seriously considered for commercial purposes and companies are being formed for that end. Ballooning is one of the popular sports in France and is indulged in by the members of both sexes.

In Paris one may secure for a small cost, a ride in a cut loose balloon accompanied by an experienced pilot, to some distant point. Many French people own their own balloons and make flights whenever they desire.

It is a common sight in Paris to see a balloon or dirigible flying across the city dropping bags of sand or emitting clouds of smoke from the motor exhaust. Various forms and kinds of dirigible balloons are produced in Paris. Most of them are not unlike those seen in our own country, except that those in France are larger than ours.

The cigar shaped bag with a long framework beneath for the motor and passengers seems to be the most general design. Lately the Malcot airship has made its appearance in Paris. This airship is a combination of balloon and aeroplane driven by a gasoline motor. The bag is cigar shaped and has a sort of car suspended immediately beneath it which carries the machinery and passengers. Between the bag and car is a fixed plane extending the length of the bag. Also suspended by a long rope beneath the car is a basket which is filled with ballast or a passenger and is arranged so as to be moved forward or backward causing the airship to tip up or down thus varying the degrees of inclination of the planes. This arrangement allows the raising and lowering of the airship without the loss of gas or ballast so long as it is in motion. It is a very desirable feature but has the disadvantage of being useless when the ship is not in motion as planes or rudders have no effect except when in motion and their efficiency is proportionate to the speed they travel. The Malcot dirigible is propelled by a single motor which drives two propellers placed one on each side of the car and slightly above it. The ordinary rudder is used for turning.

This dirigible has been making successful trips but has yet to demonstrate any superiority over the ordinary types.

To Germany belongs the honor of having produced the most successful airships: that of Count Zeppelin being foremost and largest. The ill-fated Zeppelin dirigible, which was built originally for the German government, was destroyed by lightning at Mayance. It was 410 feet long and 30 feet in diameter. It carried two 120 horsepower Pauhard motors which drove two propellers each and was controlled, like the Malcot with rudders and planes. Two cars each holding 7 people were attached to the bag, one at each end. These cars were connected by a small walk way and a complete telephone system. The Zeppelin type of gas bag is stiffened by an interior construction of aluminum and is divided into 18 different compartments each separate and by this arrangement is made almost impossible to burst.

The disaster to the Zeppelin airship of California could never have happened to a bag of the Morrell type.

To the present date the Zeppelin holds the record for time and distance in the air.

HEAVIER-THAN-AIR MACHINES

The aeroplane bids fair to become the prevailing type of air craft in the future, for many reasons chief of which are its ability to fly faster against the wind, its speed and cheapness of construction. Aeroplanes guaranteed to fly are now being sold in France for $1,000 to $5,000.

The immense factory of the Vosin Bros at Ballincourt, near Paris, is entirely devoted to the building of heavier-than-air machines and they are being kept busy night and day trying to supply the demand for this new form of locomotion. In France there are at present about one hundred different aeroplanes which may be seen in operation on the military grounds around Paris and other cities.

The Wright Bros. are now taking orders and getting ready to deliver their type of aeroplane for $1,000 and $5,000—a large and a small machine.

The Vosin type of machine, as used by Farman and Delarauge, is probably the most used type at present and is also the most stable and easy to handle but is more dangerous in side winds and sudden gusts.

The monoplane or single plane type is destined to become the most popular in the future according to those who have tried them. It is true the monoplane has not yet given the results that the double plane type has, but this is due more to its not being developed as thoroughly as the biplane. The monoplane is cheaper and more easily constructed and is faster in the air besides leaving the ground more quickly after the start.

Bleriot, who began his experiments with the double or biplane type has abandoned it in favor of the monoplane and has recently been able to fly 19 miles and return across the county at a high rate of speed with and against a strong changeable wind. Bleriot had numerous accidents with his monoplanes but still adheres to this type stating that it is the most preferable of all.

After witnessing the flights of all the most successful aeroplanes in Europe the writer is of the opinion that the monoplane will ultimately become the most prominent type, though not along the lines as followed by the French for the following reasons: On nearly all French planes a single propeller is used and this is revolved at a high rate of speed thus causing a fierce gyroscopic effect which interferes with the control of the aeroplane to an alarming extent and it is the belief of the writer that this one thing has been the most serious drawback to the progress of the French aeroplane.

However, since the Wright Bros. invasion of Europe with their two propellers, the French have begun to sit up and take notice, and as a result are fitting two propellers, instead of one, on all their planes.

A great thing in favor of the monoplane is that the higher the speed the less the horsepower and supporting surface needed and as the monoplane has proven the fastest of all types this is a very desirable feature in its favor. There is also a tendency to do away with the rudders and tails, etc., and simplify the control as much as possible.

The frames are generally made of ash or bamboo covered with silk or rubber cloth and braced with piano wire.

The motors are generally of the multi-cylinder type, as many as sixteen cylinders being used. This type of motor can be built with less weight per horsepower than any other type. No flywheel is used, the propeller acting in this capacity. Some of the motors of today furnish 1 horsepower to 2 lbs in weight.

The Antoinette is probably the lightest and mostly used of aeronautical motors. This motor is water cooled and has a separate carburetor for each cylinder. It is made in sizes up to sixteen cylinders.

The Renault firm is also marketing a remarkably light air cooled aeronautical motor which has been used with great success. Most of these motors use no carburetor but simply inject the gasoline into the intake pipe as needed; this method is most successful and produces a high efficiency from the motor.

The Wright Bros. motor is of their own design and manufacture and is a marvel for the purpose, being four cylinder, water cooled with jump spark ignition. A centrifugal pump on the crankshaft circulates the water through very large pipes to the radiator. A pump level splash system of lubrication is used and the gasoline is injected into the intake pipe as needed, no carburetor being used.

In the operation of the different aeroplanes, the writer has noticed that with the Farman and Delarauge type there is great difficulty in getting off the ground and sometimes hours are spent trying to make a flight. The multi-cylinder high speed motors are always balking and continually misfiring. In the Vosin type of plane the speed decreases very considerably on the turns and while turning a heavy gust of wind sometimes brings it to the earth. Also the Vosin Type seems to be more affected by side winds than the single planes.

With the Wright Bros. biplane the decrease on the turns is not so noticeable but they are constantly pitching and tossing in the varying winds as against the steady flying of the Vosin type and monoplane. The Wright machine is more easily handled by the operator but has to be continually kept right by the driver.

In conclusion it is the opinion of the writer that the future successful aeroplane will be a monoplane with two or more propellers and small sustaining surface and horsepower. It will have automatic control and stability in addition to the control of the operator and will be fitted with clutches to release the motor and let it run when a landing is made so as to have power ready should anything happen to prevent a landing, etc.

It is hoped that the recent successful performances of experimenters in this and other countries will stimulate the progress of aerial navigation to such an extent as to put the United States to thinking and send her ahead in this, the greatest of coming industries.

By the time Robinson had returned to St. Louis, he had become obsessed with building his own airplane. He was now convinced that the single-wing monoplane was the design of the future, despite the fact that many airplane builders disagreed and continued to construct multiwinged aircraft.

Robinson began to build scaled-down models of the aircraft he would eventually name the Flyer (fig. 10). As he experimented with models, he learned through trial and error. In early 1909 he finally built his monoplane with the propeller in front of the engine and the pilot's place behind. This arrangement was the reverse of all pusher types, including the

10. *This monoplane, which Robinson built in 1909 and called the Flyer, was the culmi-
nation of all the ideas he gathered on his seven-thousand-mile trip through Europe in
1908. He wrote to his mother about the model, "On this base lie my future hopes!" The
influence of the Wright brothers is clear in the twin propellers that turn in opposite di-
rections to push the craft forward.*

Wright aircraft, in which the pilot sat in front of the engine and the propeller pushed from the rear. The Flyer (fig. 11) had a twenty-three-horse-
power engine that Robinson had designed and built himself. This engine
produced one unit of horsepower to two and a half pounds of weight. The
monoplane was 34 feet long with a wing area of 240 square feet. It was
expected to fly at forty-five miles per hour. His water-cooled engine would
have to be changed to an air-cooled engine to lighten the craft's weight. It
was little more than a grass cutter.

A St. Louis newspaperman wrote in 1908, "After spending eight months
in Europe studying the methods of foreign inventors, H. A. Robinson of

1720 N. Whittier Street has successfully tried out his own aeroplane models and is now constructing a Flyer of the monoplane type with which he will attempt to travel the air next month." The writer went on to explain as well as he could how this new monoplane would also have a method for automatic stability that the pilot had not fully explained. Robinson was experimenting with Glenn Curtiss's concept of wing ailerons. These are clearly shown in the early photo of Robinson sitting at the controls of his Flyer. Later he explained how the controls operated. In those days the application of ailerons provided the pilot with adjustments in balance as he flew straight ahead, thus preventing crashes from a lack of wing control.

11. Robinson at the controls of the Flyer. There appears to be an aileron, used for lateral control, on the end of the wing. Had Robinson persisted in flying this monoplane for prize money, the Wright brothers would have sued him, as they did Glenn Curtiss, for patent infringement. They believed they had patented the aileron concept.

The article continued: "The supporting surface is constructed of varnished silk stretched over spruce and braced with piano wire." The writer further explained, "The new water-cooled engine has no carburetor but is fuel injected by a small plunger geared into the cylinders. The feature does away with the carburetor trouble in flying rarefied atmosphere."

The completed airplane weighed only 750 pounds. The V-shaped fuselage held one person: the pilot. Three fragile wheels were used for support on the ground. The controls were complicated: There was one stick for the rudder, one for the ailerons, and one for the elevators. The first trials were made in May and June of 1909 and were not successful. The four-cylinder, eighteen- to twenty-horsepower engine was not powerful enough, and the flat-bladed wood propeller could not pull hard enough to make the plane fly because it lacked the proper pitch. Robinson designed a metal propeller made of sheet aluminum and tubing. This was one of the world's first all-metal propellers. Many modifications had to be made to the entire aircraft. One was air cooling for the engine, which reduced the problem of dead weight. With these changes, Robinson was able to make short hops of a hundred to two hundred feet.

Hugh Robinson and Glenn Curtiss were both listed as fliers at the October 1909 St. Louis Centennial Exposition (fig. 12). This was the first paid exhibition flight in this country. Robinson received a hundred dollars to exhibit and fly his monoplane. Curtiss was paid a thousand dollars to attempt to fly his famous pusher airplane, with which he had won the greatest international air show in the world at Rheims, France, earlier that year.

At the show, Curtiss noticed Robinson struggling to get his monoplane into the air. Walking over to Robinson, Curtiss offered him one of his wood propellers, which had better pitch. Robinson graciously accepted. With the wood propeller, Robinson succeeded for the first time in making three short flights, all straight ahead. Though none made it farther than the end of the field, Robinson was elated with his monoplane, even though his metal propeller had been a failure.

12. Robinson's Flyer at the 1909 St. Louis Centennial Exposition, where Robinson and Glenn Curtiss met. After Curtiss observed Robinson unsuccessfully struggling to get his plane off the ground, he offered Robinson a wood propeller. After attaching the new propeller, Robinson made his first successful flights. Curtiss offered Robinson a job as his chief pilot and engineer, but only after the Flyer was wrecked in a windstorm did Robinson and his family join Curtiss in Los Angeles, California.

Impressed with Robinson as an engineer-inventor and pilot, Curtiss offered him a job as his chief pilot and engineer at San Diego, California, working on the design of the newly conceived Curtiss Hydroaeroplane and teaching the first U.S. Navy and Army pilots to fly. To be offered a job by one of the world's most famous pilots was extremely flattering, but Robinson hesitated to make a decision. He had great plans for the future of his own monoplane. He had built a new wooden laminated spruce propeller and installed a thirty- to forty-horsepower Eldridge engine for more power. The monoplane was moved to East St. Louis, where a field had been secured and a big tent erected as a hangar. Unfortunately, fate intervened: a windstorm blew down the tent and wrecked all the airplanes inside the hangar, including Robinson's monoplane. It was then that he decided to go to California and work for Curtiss.

13. *Robinson familiarizing himself with the controls of fellow airman Tom Benoist's Curtiss pusher before leaving for California. Robinson wanted to fly the plane, to familiarize himself with the Curtiss design, but a part had been misplaced in transit.*

Before leaving St. Louis, Robinson wanted to try out Tom Benoist's newly acquired Curtiss pusher (fig. 13), but the airplane was inoperable because a part had been misplaced in transit. This was a big disappointment to Robinson since he had hoped to be familiar with one of Curtiss's biplanes in flight before joining him in California. Instead, he had to settle for playing with the controls.

After resigning his job with the Dorris Motor Company, Robinson set out with his wife and sons for California.

C H A P T E R   3

Los Angeles and San Francisco, 1910–1911

Robinson joined Glenn Curtiss in Los Angeles, where Curtiss was participating in the Second International Aviation Meet at Dominguez Field, held from December 24, 1910, through January 3, 1911, and sponsored by the Los Angeles chapter of the Aero Club of America.

The pilot who was to fly the Curtiss airplane became ill, and Curtiss asked Robinson to take his place. Curtiss felt Robinson had gained sufficient experience flying his monoplane, the Flyer, in St. Louis to qualify, and Robinson agreed.

It was remarkable that Robinson had such apparent confidence in flying the Curtiss pusher in front of thousands of viewers at the air show considering that he had no experience in the air with this model. His only flying experience consisted of short hops in his monoplane after hours of trying to become airborne. After reading the one-page flight manual, he climbed into the pilot's seat and managed to take off. The flight lasted thirteen minutes before the engine died and he glided the pusher in for a landing. The possibility of being killed in a crash did not occur to him.

Robinson won $1,333.13 for one of the luckiest flights he would ever make. The number 13 was painted on the radiator of his airplane from that time on, and with few exceptions, he would not fly unless that number was there (fig. 14). An interesting facet of this number's importance to Robinson is that he had been born on Friday the 13th.

14. *Robinson at the controls of the Curtiss pusher soon after joining Curtiss at the Second International Aviation Meet, held at Dominguez Field in Los Angeles in December 1910 and January 1911. Note the rod yoke around Robinson's shoulders, which controlled the ailerons. At this meet Robinson made his first-ever flight in the pusher, winning $1333.13. Thirteen became Robinson's lucky number and is visible on the radiator of the plane. At this meet Curtiss accepted an offer to move his operation to San Diego.*

Robinson and Curtiss' well-known aviator, Eugene Ely, flew in the remainder of the Los Angeles Aviation Meet with tremendous success, and large crowds attended the gathering—most of them wondering if the planes could actually remain airborne. Biting the wind with their teeth, the aeronautic daredevils thrilled their audience by taking their bamboo and silk contraptions up to heights of twenty-five-hundred feet.

The basic Curtiss pusher biplane had two wings—one above and one below the fuselage. It had a wooden propeller and a six-cylinder engine. The pilot sat in front of the engine, where there were fewer fumes and less oil and noise. Varnished silk covered the plane's wings and tail, and the wooden frame was supported by bamboo and held together with piano wire. It was necessary for the pilot to wear earmuffs stuffed with cotton to muffle the engine's noise and goggles for eye protection against dirt and flying objects.

There was a long bamboo pole that protruded forward from the steering wheel and was attached to the box-like forward elevator, called the canard, and then attached by cable from the steering column to the horizontal surface of the tail. When a pilot pushed the wheel forward, the canard went down, causing the plane's nose to drop; simultaneously, the horizontal surface of the tail would lift, causing the plane to lose altitude. Conversely, if the wheel was pulled back, the canard went up, causing the nose to go up. The tail would then drop, causing the plane to gain altitude. The tubular frame around the pilot's shoulder controlled the ailerons, located between each set of wings at their tips. This placement of the ailerons provided stability while the plane was airborne. The same familiar body posture used in turning a motorcycle or bicycle was used for turning the aeroplane. If the pilot leaned to his left, his shoulder would push the tubular frame to the left, causing the ailerons to force the right wingtip upward. Simultaneous turning of the control wheel swung the rear of the airplane around so that a smooth left turn would be made. Leaning to the right and turning the control wheel to the right would turn the airplane to the right. The right front pedal pushed a rod against the front wheel that acted as a weak brake, while the left front pedal controlled the throttle. The pilot sat on a flat board, with only a seat belt to prevent him from being thrown from the plane in the event of an accident. The total weight of the Curtiss pusher was approximately 750 pounds. Flying the machine was a highly improvisatory activity, as the 1911 flight manual attests:

> 1) The aeronaut should seat himself in the apparatus, and secure himself firmly to the chair by means of the strap provided. On the attendant crying "Contact" the aeronaut should close the switch which supplies

electrical current to the motor, thus enabling the attendant to set the same in motion.

2) Opening the control valve of the motor, the aeronaut should at the same time firmly grasp the vertical stick or control pole which is to be found directly before the chair. The power from the motor will cause the device to roll gently forward and the aeronaut should govern its direction of motion by use of the rudder bars.

3) When the mechanism is facing into the wind, the aeronaut should open the control valve of the motor to its fullest extent, at the same time pulling the control pole gently toward his (the aeronaut's) middle anatomy.

4) When sufficient speed has been attained the device will leave the ground and assume the position of aeronautical ascent.

5) Should the aeronaut decide to return to terra firma, he should close the control valve of the motor. This will cause the apparatus to assume what is known as the "gliding position," except in the case of those flying machines which are inherently unstable. These latter will assume the position known as "involuntary spin" and will return to the earth without further action of the part of the aeronaut.

6) On approaching closely the chosen field or terrain, the aeronaut should move the control pole gently toward himself, thus causing the mechanism to alight more or less gently on terra firma.

D. C. Collier of *Collier's Magazine* was president of the San Diego chapter of the Aero Club of America. He convinced Curtiss to move the Curtiss Los Angeles Aviation Camp to North Island, across the bay from San Diego, where the balmy weather was perfect for flying. After the Los Angeles air show ended, Curtiss dismantled his camp and headed to North Island.

Meanwhile, Curtiss sent Hugh Robinson and Eugene Ely to San Francisco to fly in a meet at the Presidio (fig. 15). There Robinson flew the Curtiss pusher around the course five times to win the prize money. He was quickly improving his skills in flying this new airplane. Some of the other pilots protested Robinson's amateur status, claiming that his previous flying experiences back in St. Louis had qualified him as a professional pilot. "My experience back East in a monoplane was entirely differ-

15. The packed grandstand at the San Francisco aviation meet, January 1911, which Robinson and pilot Eugene Ely attended immediately after the Los Angeles meet. The Wright brothers' catapult can be seen at far right. In the pusher, Robinson captured first place in a half-mile straightaway contest, a duration flight contest, and two speed events, winning $3000.00 in prize money. In the duration contest he remained aloft more than fourteen minutes and ascended to a height of more than two thousand feet.

ent than with the pusher," Robinson argued, refusing to back down. "I also took only four jumps at Los Angeles to get the feel of the ship!" Then he reminded the other pilots that a biplane had already crashed at the meet and that they could use a pilot with some experience to please the crowd. "Experience is nothing to hold against an aviator," he replied sharply.

Robinson was right, and the disgruntled pilots gave up. He was permitted to fly for prize money, and his exploits at the air show were best told by this brief account in a San Francisco newspaper: "Robinson made a series of flights during the entire meet, but in the comparatively short time won prizes aggregating about $3,000. He captured the half-mile straightaway, the duration flight contest, plus two speed events. In the duration contest he stayed up over 14 minutes and ascended to a height of more than 2,200 feet."

Robinson was elated by his successful flights. The article continued, quoting Robinson: "I could have gone up to 5000 feet, but my new engine was working poorly." Robinson noted further, "I intended to remain in the air without alighting for about a half hour, but on account of my engine I did not risk it. Part of the time it was going on five cylinders and then it would jump to six, then back to five again. I decided to take no chances. It was not running right, or I could have done better. As soon as the cylinders began acting up, I decided to alight. At that . . . I came damn near going into the water!"

Immediately following the San Francisco air meet, Robinson began the design and construction of the apparatus that would allow an airplane to land on the deck of the battleship USS *Pennsylvania*, which was moored in the harbor. Eugene Ely had already demonstrated that his Curtiss airplane could take off from a ship when hoisted aboard by a crane and fly off the deck using a special takeoff platform. Although Ely had performed the takeoff in 1910 at Norfolk, Virginia, never had an aircraft landed on a battleship. Curtiss admitted to Robinson that he had no idea how to stop the plane once it landed, and he felt that it was too risky to try. Nevertheless, he allowed the experiment to proceed because he realized the great potential this maneuver could have if it could be performed successfully.

Robinson knew exactly how to stop the plane once aboard the *Pennsylvania's* rear deck. He remembered his Missouri circus experiences when he had invented a device to stop his small bicycle in his loop-the-loop Circle of Death, using ropes and sandbags inside the circus tent. Robinson knew he could adapt his invention to stopping an aircraft once it had landed on the deck of a ship. He wrote the following in his records:

> The U.S.S. Pennsylvania was anchored in San Francisco Bay. We surveyed the ship and determined the rear deck would be the best spot to erect our platform. I immediately had workmen construct a wooden deck

that was 60 feet long and 30 feet wide. The platform stuck out a few feet over the stern of the vessel giving Ely plenty of room to land if he made a perfect landing. After the platform was ready, I ordered three large U-shaped iron hooks to be made especially for the plane. Each hook was fastened to a spring device on the underside of the plane so that it extended straight down, but would flatten out horizontally to the U-shape when landing and scoop up anything in its path. Next we obtained 42 duffel bags from the ships store and filled each bag with sand so that it weighed about 50 pounds. We tied the bags together with half-inch rope and stretched them across the platform about four inches off the deck so that the U-shaped hooks would grab them. We used two, two-by-four inch boards on their sides about 20 feet apart. At the end, we built a large canvas stopper to halt Ely if he missed the hooks. Also, there were two guard rails erected by us on each side of the platform.

Robinson's plan elicited wild betting among those aboard ship. Knowing his idea would work, however, he stubbornly waited for Ely to land on the ship—upwind. The sailors were lining the rails. Everything that could be done had been done. But Ely developed engine problems ashore and left much later than his scheduled 2:30 P.M. takeoff from the Presidio, six miles away. There was a tide shift along the keel of the big ship, and it was impossible to keep the vessel from hanging directly cross-wind. Robinson knew this could be disastrous for Ely, and he scanned the sky, praying he would not see a dot on the horizon.

When Ely finally appeared, the ship had turned, thus creating a tailwind—the opposite of what was desperately needed for landing an aircraft on a ship (fig. 16).

"I waved to him to head off," reported Robinson. "All I can remember is that Ely looked as if he had two heads. Ely turned off his engine and glided in. I prayed he wouldn't overshoot the platform. He came in fast, picked up the 11th rope after missing the first 10, carrying all the hooked ropes with him two feet short of the canvas. I ran up to Ely and he was as

16. (facing page, top) Eugene Ely achieved the first aircraft landing on a ship, the USS Pennsylvania, on January 18, 1911. Robinson devised the arresting-gear system used to stop the plane; the concept is still used for landings on modern aircraft carriers. In this version, forty-two duffel bags were filled with sand and tied together with ropes stretching across a thirty- by sixty-foot landing platform. The ropes were positioned to catch a hook (the arresting gear) under the seat of the plane. Ely caught the eleventh rope and dragged the bags to within two feet of a canvas stopper erected at the end of the platform. Robinson later admitted, "I'll tell you, my heart was in my mouth until he had safely landed."

17. (facing page, bottom) Ely, Robinson, and the Curtiss pusher share the spotlight after the historic landing. Ely is the figure wearing a crossed bicycle inner tube, which he used as a life jacket. Robinson is standing at left accepting the congratulations of the sailors.

18. (above) Ely heading back to shore after his historic landing.

white as a ghost and completely speechless for a few minutes. Then we all laughed. I realized that the illusion of two heads was created by an inflated bicycle tube used as a life preserver that had a weak spot which bulged out" (fig. 17).

"I could hardly fly with that thing on my neck, but I wasn't about to burst it," yelled Ely. "I can't swim!"

"I'll tell you, my heart was in my mouth until he had safely landed," Robinson later admitted. Ely got back into the airplane and flew off the ship's deck, heading back to home base (fig. 18).

The Navy was exhilarated. Robinson, however, was content merely knowing he had made aviation history. It never occurred to him to patent the device he had created from ropes and duffel bags. Had he done so, he could have made millions, as the same principle of landing aircraft on ships is still used today.

The *Saint Louis Post-Dispatch* told the story as follows on February 5, 1911:

ST. LOUISIAN'S IDEA LANDS AEROPLANE
ON WARSHIP DECK

Hugh A. Robinson's Device Used on the
Pennsylvania Proves Value to the Navy.

JOINS CURTISS' STAFF

Former Parachute Jumper Studied
Manufacture of Flying Machines in Paris.

The aeroplane experimenters at Kinloch Field are enthusiastic over word received from the Pacific Coast that Hugh A. Robinson, formerly a member of the little camp and now one of Glenn Curtiss' aviators, was the inventor of the device for landing an aeroplane on the deck of a battleship. It was this device Eugene Ely used in his remarkable flight over San Francisco Bay to the deck of the *Pennsylvania*, which attracted worldwide attention. Robinson built an aeroplane of his own here, but was unsuccessful in his efforts to make it fly. Two months ago he accepted an offer from Glenn Curtiss and is now flying at different meets on the Pacific Coast.

When Robinson joined Curtiss, the famous aviator was conferring with navy officials on the possibilities of the aeroplane as an adjunct to the fighting armament of battleships.

The Navy officials told Curtiss that if he could land an aeroplane safely on the deck of one of their ships they would admit that the aeroplane had arrived as an instrument of naval warfare. Curtiss had previously demonstrated that his aeroplanes could rise from a specially prepared platform on a ship, but he was at a loss as to how to provide for a safe landing.

Robinson suggested placing a double line of sandbags on the platform with ropes stretched between them and placing hooks on the running gear of the aircraft that would pick up the ropes, thus gradually bringing the machine to a standstill. This device was prepared by Curtiss and used by Ely in his landing on the USS *Pennsylvania*. The aeroplane came to a stop without a jar at the end of 25 feet.

CHAPTER 4

North Island Camp, Coronado Island, California, January–April 1911

The new Curtiss Aviation Camp was located about a mile across the bay from San Diego on North Island, just west of Coronado. It was believed that North Island, which was approximately two miles long and a mile and a half wide, would be perfect for flying and for the development of the hydroplane. The island had a calm bay called Spanish Bight, which was between North Island and Coronado. There were no trees, and the land was flat and barren. Wind conditions and the weather were perfect for the men's needs. A three-year lease on the property, which included a barn that would serve as a hangar, was signed by the Spreckles Company, a private enterprise that owned the land, for twenty-five dollars a year. A fifty-foot landing pier and an 880-yard runway were added later (fig. 19).

In January W. J. "Shack" Shackelford, a mechanic, and John "Jack" D. Cooper, a foreman, were brought by Curtiss from his motorcycle factory in Hammondsport, New York, to join the camp at North Island. Two crates of Curtiss pushers had already arrived by train. Damon Merrill, an expert on airframe mechanics, brought flotation gear from the Curtiss factory in Hammondsport for the new hydroplane. Hugh Robinson was to be the engineer and flight instructor, and Eugene Ely was to be on call for special flights. Glenn Curtiss was to be the overall director of operations as well as inventor, instructor, and special test pilot.

The remaining personnel on the North Island camp consisted of the

19. *North Island, across from San Diego, site of the new Curtiss Aviation Camp. Spanish Bight is to the left. Note the ships in the calm, protected water where naval aviation began in the United States. The small hay barn hangar and the airstrip can be seen in the distance. This site later became the San Diego Naval Base.*

first military airmen, a few civilian pilots, and a local mechanic, George Hallett. As part of an effort to convince the government that aviation was important to the military, Curtiss offered to train U.S. Army and Navy pilots at no cost. The government's only obligation would be to help him with the experimental work. Lt. Ted Ellyson was the student pilot for the U.S. Navy. Lt. Paul W. Beck, 2d Lt. G. E. M. Kelly, and 2d Lt. John C. Walker were the Army students (figs. 20 and 21).

Another member of the camp was a stunt pilot by the name of Harry Harkness. He was a New York millionaire who had flown several French Antoinette airplanes that he privately owned. Harkness was always on call to demonstrate his monoplane, a high-wing, sixteen-cylinder, water-

20. Robinson (left), *Curtiss* (second from left), *and the first military trainees at the Curtiss Aviation Camp: Lt. Ted "Spuds" Ellyson, the first U.S. Navy pilot* (third from left), *and 1st Lt. Paul M. Beck, the first U.S. Army pilot.*

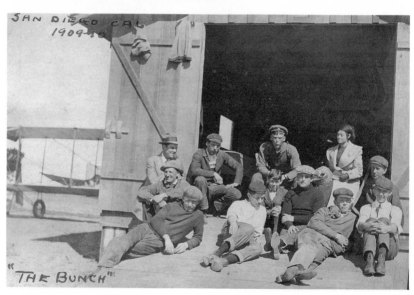

21. *The original bunch at the Curtiss Aviation Camp at North Island.* Front row, left to right: *John D. "Jack" Cooper, Lt. Ted "Spuds" Ellyson, Damon Merrill, Harold Robinson (Hugh Robinson's son), Lt. John C. Walker, 2d Lt. G. E. M. Kelly, and Hugh Robinson. Seated behind Robinson is Charles C. Witmer.* Second row, left to right: *Lt. Paul M. Beck, R. H. "Bob" St. Henry, W. J. "Shack" Shackelford, and Estia Robinson, Hugh's wife. Glenn Curtiss is absent from this photograph.*

22. *Damon Merrill (far left) was one of Curtiss's first mechanics. Hugh Robinson is at mid-wing; Jack Cooper, foreman, is touching the steering wheel. In the bowler hat is R. J. Collier, the most formally dressed of the group. Bob St. Henry, a civilian student, is leaning on the wingtip at far right next to Harry Harkness, the millionaire sportsman aviator who flew his own Antoinette planes in exhibitions at San Diego. Next is Lt. Ted Ellyson. Last is Charles C. Witmer, a civilian pilot who later started an aviation business in Miami, Florida.*

cooled, fuel-injected engine with an adjustable-pitch metal propeller. He was an excellent pilot and greatly admired by spectators for his aerobatics.

Student civilian pilots included Charles Witmer, R. H. "Bob" St. Henry, and Charles Willard. These men were training to become stunt pilots on the future Curtiss Air Exhibition Team, anticipating the large amounts of money to be made from daredevil flying. Members of the San Diego Aero Club pitched in as a group to help the new North Island Camp at San Diego get on its feet. They helped to build a runway on the jackrabbit-infested scrubland and then to remodel a hay barn to serve as a hangar and clubhouse for the pilots in training (fig. 22).

A newspaper story of that time described the North Island lease arrangements with Curtiss:

> The lease of the island is for as much ground as Curtiss shall at anytime require. The Aero Club of San Diego will erect several buildings for him, including quarters for a large force of mechanics and other workmen, new hangars, an assembling plant, machine shop, etc., and will supply electric power from the city supply. The entire plant and outfit for the Curtiss Government Aviation School will be the same as at Curtiss' Eastern Headquarters at Hammondsport, N.Y. Curtiss' aeroplanes practically will be built here. Curtiss' desire was to have his Hammondsport plant entirely shipped here, but he stated . . . that the freight rates were prohibitive.

By this time Glenn Curtiss had little money left. His motorcycle company in Hammondsport had gone into receivership, and his only remaining assets were a few pusher planes and a handful of faithful workers. Because the Curtiss operation in North Island would have to pay its own way, the team produced a flying exhibition at the aviation camp for the local townspeople. The fifty-cent ticket price included a ferry ride from San Diego and admission to the air show, which featured Curtiss, Robinson, Ely, and Harkness (fig. 23). A San Diego newspaper stated that Robinson

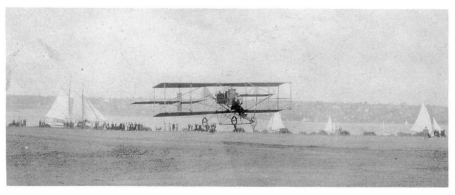

23. *Robinson performing at the North Island Air Show. Curtiss staged the show to raise money.*

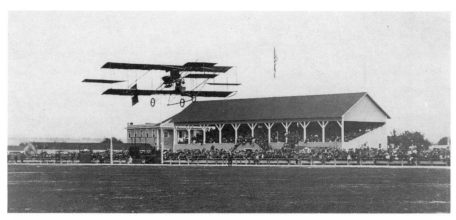

24. Robinson flying over the Coronado Hotel and polo grounds.

set a record at this show by turning his pusher to the right. Because of the gyroscopic action of the propeller, tending to pull the biplane uncontrollably to the right, all sharp turns had previously been to the left. Robinson had learned to use all of his controlling surfaces, including the tail rudder, to coordinate the turn.

The Aero Club also helped raise funds by sponsoring an aviation meet at the nearby Coronado Hotel polo grounds. The fee per person to witness this daredevil exhibition was sixty-five cents. This included the ferry, general admission, a trolley ride, and a grandstand seat (fig. 24). Air show events included a race around the polo grounds between Curtiss in his biplane and an automobile racer. After this, whenever the company needed more money to keep going, they stopped working long enough to put on a fund-raising air show.

The camp was deeply engrossed in perfecting the first hydroplane (fig. 25). In this process, a wood-frame pontoon covered with tin, built in Hammondsport, was placed under one of the Curtiss pushers. A small tin float was also placed where the front wheel was located. To keep the wings out of the water, an inflated bicycle inner tube was mounted on a flat ash roof shingle for wingtip flotation (fig. 26). Another small float had to be

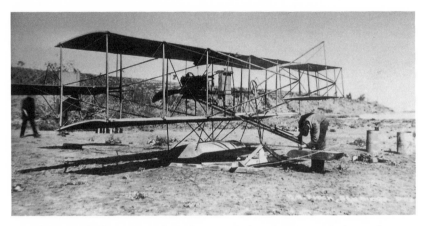

25. The Curtiss hydro prototype had a large single float that consisted of a wooden frame covered with tin. Many modifications were required before it could fly safely and reliably. In this photograph, Robinson can be seen working on the anterior nose float. Wingtip floats had not yet been installed.

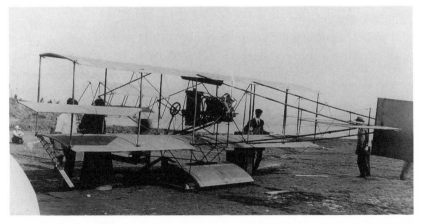

26. Curtiss is standing in front of the right wing of the hydro, Damon Merrill is behind the tail, and Robinson is in front of the left wing, pushing the plane back into the water. Note the inflated bicycle inner tubes lashed to ash shingles, used as wingtip floats to keep the wings out of the water during takeoff, taxiing, and landing.

added forward so the aircraft would plane out of the water and lift off. Many additional modifications were made, and Curtiss attempted numerous flights in his new hydroplane. Thanks to the combined efforts of all members of the camp, the hydroplane got off the water and into the air. This feat had been performed only once before—by Henri Fabre in Europe in 1909. His hydroplane was underpowered and could not fly long distances.

Curtiss finally achieved the first successful flights in the hydro off the waters of North Island on January 26. He made two flights, each lasting a minute and a half, skimming the water at forty miles per hour. They were witnessed by Colonel Collier, Harry Harkness, U.S. Army and Navy student officers, and several mechanics. Robinson witnessed both flights from shore. According to one newspaper account,

> Curtiss turned on the power and shot along the water like a flash, stirring it almost evenly at all times, and yet sending up spray that made the biplane a vertical monster flying fish. Then he pulled the forward tilting plane (canard) up and the great airship arose from the water as the little crowd on shore yelled itself hoarse in its excitement as its members realized that an unprecedented and wondrous feat of world-wide importance was taking place. Curtiss flew in short circles for about a minute and a half before attempting his water landing. He skipped along the surface before coming to a misty stop. But instead of coming ashore, he began a second flight a few minutes later. This time he flew two miles before landing safely within 100 feet of shore and the hangar. The fact that the pontoon attachments to the biplane did not seem to be submerged more than one-half their depth at any time, in rising or landing, made it evident that there was little or no element of luck in the accomplishment of the feat.

The article proclaimed to the world that Curtiss and his team had conquered for the United States the scientific challenge of taking off from water. Now that they knew the hydroplane could fly, they were faced with the challenge of making it safe and airworthy (fig. 27).

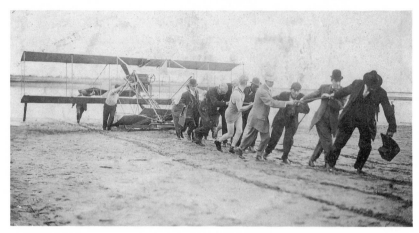

27. Led by famed publisher and magazine founder R. J. Collier, crewmen and members of the San Diego Aero Club help remove the hydro from the water. Collier was president of the club, which had induced Curtiss to set up his aviation camp at North Island.

At first the machine had no wheels and therefore had to be pulled in and out of the water on a system of "beer barrel" rollers (figs. 28 and 29) and hauled to and from the hangar many times a day as modifications were made, tested in the water, and readjusted on shore. Some of the later modifications included extending the main pontoon forward with wood and canvas for more flotation. The main float took on many shapes, from upturned bow to downturned stern (fig. 30). The craft's body also grew larger in size. Eventually the plane assumed the shape of a light scow with no upturn or downturn. A longer pontoon provided more lift. A propeller that would not splinter in the water had to be developed because the plane threw a lot of water into the air. Eventually the inventors designed a metal float for each wingtip, replacing the earlier inner tube and shingle device (fig. 31). With each new modification, further test flights had to be made, all by Curtiss. Rather than expecting his fliers to run the first tests on his newly modified airplanes, he insisted upon making these dangerous flights himself.

28. A "beer barrel" dolly was adapted to help move the hydro from the hangar into the water, but it was cumbersome and it took most of the crew to launch the plane. This procedure had to be repeated every time a modification was made onshore after testing.

29. Against the backdrop of San Diego across the bay, Curtiss, Robinson, Merrill, and the military students pull the hydro into the water. The team worked from dawn to dusk every day. At night they met to review problems and make plans for the following day.

30. The high center of thrust tended to shove the nose underwater, so a planing device was added in front of the anterior nose float to help the plane maintain the nose-up posture it needed for takeoff.

31. Final modifications combined all the separate forward planing surfaces into one single wooden pontoon and provided a metal float for each wingtip.

Robinson had always believed that the tractor design, with the pilot seated behind the engine, had its advantages (fig. 32). This plan moved the center of gravity toward the back of the aircraft, thereby helping to lift the plane into the air. Unfortunately, the pilot was deafened by the noise and invariably drenched by the spray of oil and water, so this concept was abandoned. The tractor design, however, was an important contribution to the development of the hydroplane. To show the Navy that a hydroplane could be used in conjunction with a ship at sea, Curtiss flew from North Island to the battleship USS *Pennsylvania* on San Diego Bay, where the tractor aircraft was hoisted on board. The hydroplane was placed back into the water for the return flight to North Island (fig. 33).

The need for a retractable landing gear became clear, and Curtiss, Robinson, and Damon Merrill succeeded in inventing and constructing the device, thus making their craft amphibious. With this new concept turned into reality, the hydroplane could be gunned ashore on its retractable gear, which was cranked down manually once the plane neared land. There was a wheel attached along both the right and left of the main pontoon and another smaller wheel attached to its front. Thus this version of

32. Curtiss and Robinson tried putting the pilot behind the engine with the propeller in front in what they called the tractor design.

33. *Curtiss flew the tractor-type hydro from Spanish Bight to the USS* Pennsylvania *in San Diego Bay and was hoisted aboard the ship. He was trying to show the U.S. Navy that the hydro could function as a military mechanism that could go back and forth between land and ship.*

the plane was named the Triad because of its three-point landing structure, which made it capable of performing in water and in the air as well as on land (fig. 34).

On February 4, Curtiss made a successful flight in the Triad for the first time, demonstrating the plane's practicality by flying to the Coronado Hotel to have lunch with his wife (fig. 35). The retractable gear allowed him to beach the hydroplane behind the hotel while they dined. When they were finished with lunch, he started the engine, rolled into the water, and then pulled up the landing gear and took off for his return to camp.

In addition to the problem of money, the company had to keep trying to convince the public as well as the government that there was a practical

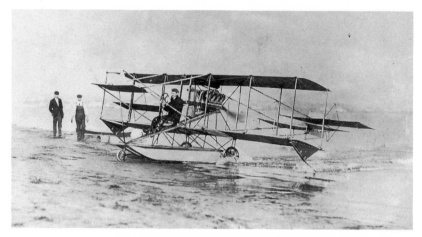

34. Because of design improvements over the previous version, the triad version of the Curtiss hydro was easier to launch and to retrieve from the water.

35. Curtiss landing the triad on the beach at the Coronado Hotel.

36. Robinson introduced the concept of dive-bombing to the military and public on April 2, 1911. For this maneuver, a mock fort was constructed of boxes and canvas on the polo grounds of the Coronado Hotel. As he flew over the fort, Robinson dropped simulated bombs that penetrated the fort's walls and made the soldiers scatter.

use for aviation in general and the hydroplane in particular. This was the work these dedicated men were destined to do, and they savored every moment of their mission. They knew they were on a new frontier in aviation in making an airplane that could be used on both water and land.

To help demonstrate the hydroplane's importance, Robinson pioneered military dive-bombing at an aviation meet on April 2 at the Coronado Hotel polo grounds. He had a mock fort of boxes and canvas boards constructed. It held several hundred soldiers, a large cannon, and guns with blank ammunition (fig. 36). The purpose of the dive-bombing was to produce much smoke and noise and demonstrate that Robinson could blow San Diego off the map if he chose to do so. To add to the thrill of this aerial assault demonstration, ground soldiers were allowed to touch off preset blasts at will if the bombardment did not hit the explosive targets.

By direct wire to the *Los Angeles Times*, a reporter was pulled from his regular city hall job to become one of America's unnamed early aviation writers. "Land Forces Suffer," declared his April 2 headline, followed by the line "Aviation Meet closed with bombardment of oranges." Here is most of his story about Robinson's aerial attack:

> The farewell aviation meet of the San Diego Aero Club for the season at the Coronado Country Club today was a spectacular bombardment of a miniature fort of canvas boards and boxes. These were mined (predetermined blast set-ups) and from a height of several hundred feet aviator R. H. [sic] Robinson, in a Curtiss Machine (the Hydro), dropped oranges which, when they landed on the right spot, touched off a mine. Though not as realistic as a pure enough bombardment, by pre-arranged methods, enough smoke and noise were produced to compel the spectators to believe that aeroplanes can be classed as formidable weapons of destruction. Robinson was in the air fifteen or twenty minutes during which period, besides the oranges, he threw out imitation bombs that exploded in the air and sustained the promise made beforehand that this flight would be spectacular. The attack on the fort was not without a defense. Several hundred soldiers, both regulars and the militia, did their best to take pot shots at the demon bird flying beyond range of the imaginary shots of their rifles. The soldiers, however, were obliged to seek for safety when a bombardment of bombs began to crumble the walls of canvas and which were susceptible to ignition from the blazing missiles. Short flights were made by Lt. Theodore G. Ellyson of the United States Navy and C. G. Witmer, both pupils of Glenn Curtiss. Because of a high wind, their efforts were not of a spectacular nature.

What this early aviation writer failed to understand was that dive-bombing from a Curtiss pusher was an almost impossible feat. The pilot's hands and feet, as well as his body movements, were used to guide the plane. Ejecting oranges while the plane was pointed toward the ground at a steep angle required taking at least one hand off the control wheel. Because Curtiss and Robinson believed such stunts were extremely important in convincing the military that there was a place for aviation in warfare, they were willing to take the risk.

The hours the men spent in practice and regular flights spawned another local news clipping. This was a tongue-in-cheek injunction that was supposedly served on the famous Glenn Curtiss on March 6. "I have been enjoined from flying over here anymore," the aviator complained, feigning a long face and showing the reporter his injunction for cease-and-desist measures on Spanish Bight:

> Therefore, this is to command you, your counselors, your attorneys, solicitors, servants, agents and employees, and all others acting in and of assistance of you, and each and every one of you, to absolutely desist and refrain from disturbing the peace and quietude of the inhabitants of Spanish Bight by the use of a queer contrivance which emits queer noises and odiferous odors, causing said inhabitants to seemingly and uselessly vacate our place of abode, and otherwise disturbing our solitude. Further, we enjoin you from the use of certain devices of wing warping and lateral stability, and of certain other designs for rising from water and alighting on land. For rising from land and alighting on water. M.U.D. Hen enjoins you from the use of his method of leaving water, and H.E.L.L. Diver believes your method of diving to be a direct infringement on his method of diving. In as much as he needs no assistance to the surface, he is inclined to allow you this privilege out of kindness of heart, believing it is no infringement of his patent rights.

> > Signed:
> > M. Seal
> > M. Butterball
> > E. T. Canvasback
> > M. Sprigg
> > C. Gull
> > A. Flying Fish
> > J. Porpoise
> > H.E.L.L. Diver
> > O. U. Stingray

> All citizens of Spanish Bight Attest:
> > Judge B.I.G. Pelican

Shortly after this whimsical letter was written, Curtiss made the first passenger-carrying flight. With Lt. Ellyson on board beside him, he flew the Triad across Spanish Bight, rising to a height of about a hundred feet and remaining aloft for nearly five minutes. Along with Curtiss and Ellyson and their gear, the hydroplane carried an additional four hundred pounds in cargo.

Robinson, Ellyson, and a camp mechanic surpassed this accomplishment by carrying two passengers aboard the Curtiss pusher. The Curtiss biplane's fifty-horsepower engine was able to handle the extra weight and circled North Island at a height of fifty feet. In 1911 this was clearly an advancement into aircraft passenger-carrying capabilities, and the breakthrough served to open opportunities in commercial flying. "It was really steadier in the air with two passengers," replied Robinson on landing. "Much easier to fly than with only one person" (fig. 37).

37. Robinson took students Kelly and Walker up on a flight that proved to the military that the airplane could carry heavy loads and passengers.

On March 26 Hugh Robinson and Charles Willard were sent to San Bernadino, California, where they put on a spectacular air show before large crowds. The potential for raising money by stunt flying became even more apparent with the success of this exhibition.

In training, both the military and civilian flight students would arise at dawn and "cut grass" with the pushers when there was little or no wind on the flat terrain. The treeless, rather drab area came alive with pushers taxiing back and forth under the student pilots' hands. There were governors on the throttles, and the pitch of the propellers was almost flat so that the airplanes could not attain enough lift to get off the ground. According to one of the mechanics, this was "just in case someone might feel his oats and try to solo."

Robinson supervised the ground exercises, along with classroom flight training, which allowed the entire band of students to learn the feel of the rudder and ailerons before taking off into the air on their own. The only accident that occurred on takeoff happened when Ellyson's aircraft did a ground loop because he weighed so little. The plane crashed, but Ellyson was only slightly injured. As the students progressed, their instructor gave them more and more power by adjusting the governors on the throttles and increasing propeller pitch. First they made short hops, or "jumps" as Hugh called them, and later short solo flights.

By March 11 they had all graduated to the larger eight-cylinder pusher. As Robinson had discovered at previous air shows, this plane was very difficult to fly. He gave his students all the advice he could, but little was known about this aircraft at the time. A local newspaper article revealed some of the experiences and thoughts of the new pilots as they advanced to this next step in their training:

> "I thought for a minute that I would have to either make a turn or suddenly appear in the camp of my regiment on Point Loma," said Lt. Kelly.
>
> "I pushed the front elevator down as far as it would go, but the machine continued to rise, and there was nothing to do but stay with it and try to coax it to settle."

An air of expectancy prevails in the army squad and none of the students would be surprised to be ordered to the Mexican boundary for patrol duties and actual aerial scouting. They argued that while they do not consider themselves sufficiently skilled in handling airplanes, the war department will not stop to consider their lives in case of an emergency.

While the country was not at war, the Army considered planes excellent for border patrols, as Mexican revolutions seethed and U.S. troops occupied Veracruz.

For about three months the students took the pushers apart and then put them back together again. They were taught to make almost any repair, including overhauling the entire engine. Curtiss and Robinson knew that in order for the students to be good aviators, they would have to be good mechanics and to understand every facet of their airplanes. In time the students graduated from the four-cylinder to the more powerful and harder to control eight-cylinder biplane.

When Curtiss thought the hydroplane was safe enough for students, he and Robinson, who had become proficient in flying the craft, began to teach them how to fly it. Their lessons began with the required pontoon ride so that they could get the feel of taking off from the water. Some wondered if they might drown in the process. Then came the first hydroplane accident at North Island.

A news story reported: "Pontoon wrecked—Hydroaeroplane goes to Davy Jones' Locker." It described the flight of Curtiss in the hydroplane with Witmer riding on the float beneath. Trying to land on the water of Spanish Bight after he had shut down his engine, Curtiss descended at too steep an angle, striking the water with force sufficient to split the sides of the pontoon. The pontoon immediately filled with water and sank below the surface. As always happened, the propeller was destroyed upon striking the water.

Wittmer extricated himself from the wreckage, and a small fleet of motorboats and rowboats arrived. The rescuers found the two men laughing at themselves and each other. The minor accident was considered a positive sign, because it was the first mishap in weeks of experimentation and had taken place in a new apparatus. The accident led to the design of a new pontoon made of many small compartments acting as air pockets, an improvement that increased flotation capability in case of an accident.

In April the government finally ordered two Curtiss airplanes. One was a pusher with a high-powered engine. The other was a two-man hydro, named the A-1, that could be altered to serve as a land plane like the Triad with its three wheels, making it amphibious. The pusher was to be for the Army's use and the hydro for the Navy's use. This government purchase signified the beginning of American military aviation, which was considerably behind Europe's advances in this field at that time.

In mid-1911 the Army sent its first pusher and a Bleriot plane from France to the Texas-Mexican border to patrol the eighteen hundred miles of unprotected land there. Thus the first military operation was launched, with Lt. Charles Hamilton flying the pusher and Roland Garros in the French plane. The Navy hydroplane, which had been purchased for ten thousand dollars, was flown by Lt. Ellyson, who made history as the Navy's first pilot.

The military A-1 hydroplane, accompanied by Lt. Ellyson, was taken back to Hammondsport, New York, for final modifications required by the U.S. Navy. This Curtiss hydroplane was the primary achievement of the North Island Camp and was destined to see military duty. It had a wingspan of thirty feet and was powered by an eight-cylinder, sixty-horsepower water-cooled engine that flew at sixty miles per hour carrying 175 pounds. It was also adapted for carrying two persons, either of whom could fly the hydroplane because of its dual controls. It flew for two hours without refueling and maneuvered on land as well as in the water by virtue of its hand-operated retractable landing gear.

In April Curtiss was able to recover his Hammondsport factory from receivership. Because his presence was required there, he hurried to complete his work at North Island. Lt. Ellyson had been assigned to him at

Hammondsport for further training, while Army pilots Walker, Beck, and Kelly were posted for maneuvers in San Antonio, Texas. Hugh Robinson arranged to join the newly formed daredevil Curtiss Exhibition Team.

On the whole, Glenn Curtiss received well-deserved recognition for his accomplishments in California. Alexander Graham Bell, the inventor of the telephone, should also be given credit for teaching Curtiss the method of experimentation. Recognition was also in order for Curtiss's crew, which had worked so faithfully and effectively. In a very limited time they had all met their objectives: a Curtiss pusher had been purchased by the Army, a reliable hydroplane had been developed and sold to the Navy, and the first military pilots had been trained. Rarely in history has so much been accomplished so quickly. Their work resulted in the birth of naval aviation, the establishment of the Curtiss Aviation School at North Island, and eventually the San Diego Naval Air Station. The men were sad to leave each other when the crew disbanded from North Island in April 1911.

C H A P T E R 5

The Curtiss Exhibition Team, 1911

In an effort to make money for themselves and to help pay for further research and operations at the Curtiss home base in Hammondsport, New York, a select group of fliers formed the Curtiss Exhibition Team. The team members traveled individually or in pairs to air shows in cities throughout the United States and Canada. The exhibition pilots were preceded by their agent, Jerome Fanciulli, who arranged bookings for them and obtained important preperformance publicity.

Among the early fliers on the team were Robinson, James J. Ward, Lincoln Beachy, Charles F. Willard, Eugene Walter, Cromwell Dixon, Eli Brookins, Beckwith Havens, R. H. St. Henry, Charles Hamilton, J. A. D. McCurdy, Bud Mars, Augustus Post, Lansing Callan, C. F. Walsh, R. C. McHenry, Eugene Godet, and C. C. Witmer.

Robinson was assigned to tour with full-time mechanic W. J. Shackelford, one of Curtiss's best mechanics from Hammondsport. He was to be paid twenty-five dollars a week. Before they could begin their tour, the two men had to learn how to dismantle the pusher and pack its parts into crates for shipping by railroad to each stop on the tour. One crate contained the wings and tail; another was for miscellaneous parts such as the landing gear, wires, and cables. A third crate carried the engine, and a fourth held the tools. The heavy crates were usually transported by wagon to the railroad station, where they were placed on a

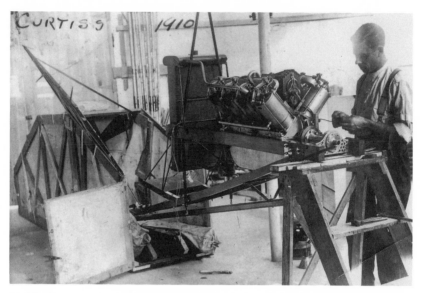

38. The Curtiss pusher being dismantled and crated for transport to an air show.

39. Robinson, fourth from left, and Shackelford, in his usual overalls, shown on the flat railroad car with the crated airplane parts.

flatbed rail car. When they arrived at their destination, they were taken to the exhibition site and the airplane was reassembled. This was a painstaking procedure, often lasting well into the night, especially if repairs were needed (figs. 38 and 39).

Robinson's first exhibition was in Rapid City, South Dakota. His wife and two sons traveled with him on the train, stopping for two days en route for Robinson to help Curtiss with an exhibition of the hydroplane in Salt Lake City. In Rapid City the pusher made quite an impression on the local townspeople as it was uncrated downtown at the Rapid City Transfer Company before being taken to the flying field. Robinson and Shackelford supervised the uncrating and heard such comments from the crowd as those quoted by the *Rapid City Journal* on April 13: "That machine looks like the only solution to tire trouble and dust nuisance" and "The workingman's automobile has come at last. . . . It wasn't too long ago one of these 'Devil Wagons' [autos] would have caused as much commotion as this flying machine. . . . Wouldn't it be great to take people out to see subdivision property in that thing!"

The Curtiss pusher was the first airplane seen in South Dakota, and the exhibition was immensely successful. On April 12 Robinson made two flights late in the day, after the crowd had assembled on the field. Messengers had combed the town ballyhooing the occasion, and people had rushed from their homes to see this exciting event. On his final wind-plagued flight, Robinson had gained an altitude of about four hundred feet when stormy weather and darkness caused him to make a forced landing in the middle of a Sioux Indian camp. As he was landing, a delivery truck drove into his path and sheared off part of one wing. Robinson was thrown clear and escaped with only minor scratches. He found himself greeted by a group of Indians in full headdress (fig. 40). "Nice for the children to see *real* Indians," commented Mrs. Robinson, taking the accident in stride. According to a local newspaper, Robinson had "reached an altitude of 300 to 400 feet and covered half to three quarters of a mile."

From Rapid City the Robinson entourage journeyed to Edmonton,

40. Robinson's forced landing among the Sioux Indians.

Canada, where Robinson made the first flights in the history of Alberta province. From April 29 to May 1 he performed at the Edmonton Horse Show grounds before a large audience that watched from both inside and outside the exhibition grounds; the event was covered by the *Edmonton Daily Journal* on May 1. Bob St. Henry flew his Curtiss pusher with Robinson at this show. He was one of the two civilian pilots of the original group who were trained by Curtiss in San Diego, and he flew purely for the money and the excitement.

The next aviation meet was held from May 4 to May 7 at the Benning Race Track in Washington, D. C. Robinson was joined there by two other pilots: J. A. D. McCurdy, an original member of the earlier Aerial Experiment Association of New York, which had developed the Curtiss pusher in 1907; and Lincoln Beachy, who was to become one of the most daring stunt pilots in the world. Robinson had met Beachy when he was flying dirigibles in St. Louis and helped teach him how to fly the Curtiss pusher.

Both Beachy and Robinson attempted to obtain their pilot's licenses while they were in Washington, D.C., in May. Beachy passed his test flight and received license number 27 from the Aero Club of America by flying a figure eight five times at an altitude of six hundred feet and landing within seven feet of a designated landing point. During Robinson's test flight, while he was over the Potomac River, his engine began to skip. He found that he could not get back to the starting point, so he selected a clear spot on the bank of the river to land on. Unfortunately, the area he chose was a deep mud hole. On landing, he and the pusher became submerged in the muck. Afraid that he was in quicksand, he jumped up to get out and hit his head on the radiator, lacerating his forehead. Fortunately, he emerged from the muddy shore with only the cut on his head. The crowd was greatly relieved, fearing that he had been killed. The biplane was removed from the mud, and Robinson and Shackelford worked through the night to get it ready for the next day's show. They were both greatly saddened that Robinson was unable to get his pilot's license because of this engine failure.

The next day Robinson flew once again in the nation's capital, carrying passengers who had won flights in a newspaper contest. The flights were a half mile in length at an altitude of fifty feet. The *New York Herald Tribune* reported that Mrs. Nicholas Longworth (Alice Roosevelt, President Theodore Roosevelt's daughter), unwilling to settle for merely a hop down the runway, had offered a hundred dollars to fly longer and higher. But Curtiss, who was in Washington that day, would not allow her to go for such a lengthy hop. He was still shaken by Robinson's crash the day before.

The Washington meet was successful and well attended. Spectators included many celebrities, congressmen, ambassadors, the Chinese and Bolivian ministers, an attaché of the Russian embassy, the secretary of war, and President Taft's former secretary, Charles D. Norton.

At his next stop, in Paducah, Kentucky, Robinson suffered a horrifying experience of the kind that had previously killed several airmen. While flying at 450 feet with no seat belt during the first day of the exhibition, he was blown out of his board seat by a gust of wind. Robinson fell forward over his steering wheel, pitching the plane into a nosedive. He managed to reach back and grab one of the radiator supports before pulling himself back into his seat. Then he brought the steering wheel back into place and pulled his airplane out of the dive. Meanwhile, the engine had died, and only the sound of wind penetrating the bamboo struts could be heard. Robinson landed too short and hit a canvas barrier at the far end of the field. Amazingly, he suffered only scratches and bruises.

Robinson's crash into the mud and his more recent air mishap were of concern to him. He promised himself that he would not fly when the wind was wrong, even if there were fifty thousand angry spectators present who might accuse him of being a phony. The pioneer pilots were men of daring who flew with no seat belts, had no protective cockpit enclosing them, and had only a small, flat piece of wood placed between them and the ground below. As a flier, Robinson was not a daredevil like Ely or Beachy. He was a man who took only calculated risks. With silk, spruce, noise, and weather in his face, he found flying itself precarious enough.

The *Paducah New Democrat* covered the exhibition extensively. The paper had sponsored the event and had therefore urged the townspeople to buy their tickets in advance at local stores to "avoid the rush that will usually take place." Stories of the air show were carried on the front page of the newspaper.

The exhibition meet was to be held at Gregory Heights Aviation Grounds, and the Paducah paper had optimistically predicted that twenty-five thousand people would attend the two-day event. When only three thousand appeared, the paper reported that thousands of persons planning to attend had been held up at railroad stations because a large Confederate convention was being held at the same time in Little Rock, Arkansas.

The next of the many exhibitions was in Chickasaw, Oklahoma, on May 23 and 24. There Robinson and James Ward, a young new member of the Curtiss Exhibition Team, put on a show for the state editors' convention (fig. 41). From there they traveled to Lincoln, Nebraska, for a May 25–26 show. Robinson flew conservatively at this meet, having just received the news that one of his students at North Island, Lt. G. E. M.

JIMMIE WARD
YOUNGEST AVIATOR
— IN THE WORLD

41. Billed as the youngest aviator in the world, James "Jimmie" Ward joined Robinson at Chickasha, Oklahoma, where the two flew for the State Editors' Convention on May 23, 1911. Ward died in a crash at the age of nineteen.

Kelly, had been killed in Texas. Kelly had apparently been thrown out of his U.S. Army pusher when he lost control of the plane while it was still on the ground. By this time Robinson was becoming more cautious every day, and the weather had to be nearly perfect for him to fly.

Several problems had begun to surface with the Curtiss pusher. Typically, the brakes were minimal, and there was no provision for steering except when the plane was moving fast enough to conduct an air flow over the surface of the rudder. Most of the time the pilot coasted or rolled to a stop or stopped the plane by hitting a barrier (fig. 42). Sometimes, in their enthusiasm, spectators would jump in front of the plane to help it come to a stop. At other times, the pilots lost engine power and would have to go down for a landing wherever they happened to be. Such a spot could be a parking lot full of cars or other obstacles. Many pilots' bones were broken in the process of landing.

The Curtiss pusher was expensive and fragile. It required constant maintenance. A complete pusher cost between forty-five hundred and six thou-

42. Sometimes the only way a pilot could stop the pusher once it landed was to crash into something solid. Since seat belts were not used, the pilot was usually hurled forward out of his seat. Pilots suffered many broken bones as a result.

sand dollars, which was a lot of money in 1911. The pusher models were equipped with four-, six-, and eight-cylinder engines that could produce from twenty-six to four hundred units of horsepower. Their weight varied between 550 to 850 pounds, depending on the size of the engine and the configuration of the airframe. The airframe itself was built of various kinds of wood and bamboo held together with tinned fasteners. The wing and control surfaces were covered with silk, canvas, or Irish linen made airtight by the application of a varnish called dope.

Robinson flew in Joplin, Missouri, on June 28 and 29 (fig. 43). Among the spectators were Robinson's mother and several of his friends from Neosho. The weather was good, and Robinson's performance was spectacular. He remembered his bicycle crash at Big Springs Hill, and he flew his best to impress his family and friends. Later, at a reception in his hometown, Robinson, being shy and introspective, had little to say. The Neosho paper quoted an old-timer who remarked, "Hugh never did talk very much, but he always performed right smart." This was as accurate a description as anyone ever made of Robinson and his mannerisms.

The team was doing its part in raising money to keep Hammondsport operating. Both Robinson and Curtiss knew that aviation was coming of age and more planes would have to be manufactured soon. And they knew there would be many changes. With their families and planes, the Curtiss Exhibition Team members moved across the country, following the railroad tracks. They did an amazing job of ground support and succeeded in keeping their air show spectators happy.

The team carried with it the tools and spare parts for repairs that were needed after each flight and often in mid-show. Struts would break; wire

43. *Robinson, cigar in hand, in Joplin, Missouri, casually bracing a bamboo support under his arm to steady the pusher while Shackelford hand-starts the engine.*

cables snapped and linen ripped. The crowd was happy only if the airmen flew. If they were unable to fly, the spectators grumbled and turned ugly, wanting their money refunded. It required toughness as well as talent to avoid accidents and entertain the large crowds, which could swing from elation to surliness. Robinson was often the butt of their disappointment and would leave the scene of such an outburst, concerned with staying alive.

Robinson's family continued to accompany him from city to city, living in hotels, covering the Midwest by train. It was difficult, but Mrs. Robinson and the boys managed it all in resignation and good humor (fig. 44). Mrs. Robinson conducted daily classes for Hugh Jr. and Harold in their private Pullman car or in whatever hotel they were staying in. Jerome Fanciulli, the advance man, continued to move ahead of the team, setting up dates, recruiting towns, and managing finances. The team was actually more of a road show, with a rally at every stop, creating the atmosphere of a circus with only the clouds for tents.

In Little Rock, Arkansas, Robinson encountered problems. During his first flight in that city, the engine sputtered and nearly stopped. Robinson managed to keep it running, however, and he made it to the flying field, which was little more than a cow pasture. Robinson set the failing Curtiss pusher down on rough ground, and his support team quickly moved in to repair the faulty engine. During his second flight, Robinson's engine failed completely, and the defeated aviator was forced to land his expensive aircraft in a farmer's field a half mile from the disappointed crowd. His landing was faultless, however, and the farmer rushed out and gave him a hearty welcome.

Robinson's account to a local newspaper quoted the farmer as saying, "This is the first time an aeroplane has ever landed on my place. It is also the first time anybody came to see me by air. I haven't anything very strong to offer you, but if you'll take some buttermilk with me, I'll be mighty glad to have you served." Robinson accepted, declaring that he had a decided liking for the frothy, old-fashioned country buttermilk. The excited farmer

44. Hugh Robinson and his family. For a while the Robinsons lived as if they were part of a circus, moving across the country from air show to air show. The planes, crated in boxes, were carried on flat railroad cars behind the family's Pullman car.

invited Robinson to use his field for future landings and to visit him any time he was in the area. Robinson hoped any future landing in this field would not be an emergency.

At that time, exhibition flights were contracted with city officials, local newspapers, chambers of commerce, or newly-formed aeronautical clubs for a sum ranging from two thousand to six thousand dollars. This was a great deal of money in a time when a complete dinner cost twenty-five cents and a cup of coffee a nickel. Sugar sold for five cents a pound, and an entire family could eat for seven dollars a week. Several thousand dollars for exhibition contracts was therefore high finance indeed, and aviation exhibitions commanded top dollar. The pilots were paid according to their abilities and the fame they had achieved, plus their track record in not wrecking their expensive planes. A beginner could earn twenty-five percent and a virtuoso pilot up to fifty percent of the take at a show. A thousand dollars was a commonplace earnings figure for a day's work, but the more famous pilots got as much as five thousand dollars a day.

These pilots were required to perform at all of the air shows, or admission fees were refunded to the purchasers. The usual admittance fee was fifty cents if the ticket was purchased in advance, seventy-five cents if it was bought at the field. Special cars, as well as trolleys, were used to transport the spectators to the exhibition grounds. Some arrived in their own automobile, and the price for parking was a dollar.

Robinson continued to refuse to fly in adverse weather. He would hold up a wet finger to test the wind, and if there was too much, he would wait for more favorable conditions. Before a flight, the crowd was allowed to examine and touch the plane as a gesture of goodwill. Some were knocked down by the force of the propellers spinning at fifteen hundred revolutions per minute. The pilots and their planes were now flying at giddy altitudes of four thousand feet and often resembled large, soaring birds. When the pilots had performed an especially death-defying feat, the spectators carried them on their shoulders as if they were war heroes (fig. 45). It seemed as if the crowds could never get enough of the fliers' daring exhibitions. The farm animals in their once serene pastures, however, took quite a different view of these antics in the air. Horses bolted in the fields, cows stampeded, and chickens became paranoid, flying in circles and refusing to lay eggs. Horses reared as they pulled their buggies and had to be tightly reined.

For the next air show, in Topeka, Kansas, in June, people traveled long distances by every available form of transportation including buggy, bicycle, and foot. The only mishap that occurred in this show was when Robinson's plane hit a downdraft and, like a feather in the wind, was thrown into the top of a tree. The motor flew off over Robinson's head and finally

45. *After a successful flight, the pilot would be the center of attraction, as Robinson is in this photograph. If for some reason the flight had to be postponed, however, the crowds would turn hostile.*

buried itself in the ground. Robinson crashed through tree limbs, breaking his collarbone and three ribs. But the next day he was back in the air.

Robinson and Ward went on to Salina, where Ward set a world record by reaching an altitude of eight thousand feet. As the fliers of this time progressed to greater altitudes, they still sat out in the open, unprotected by cockpit or windshield. While traveling east to Hammondsport from San Diego, Glenn Curtiss stopped in St. Louis, where he had promised to send Robinson for an exhibition to be scheduled in June. Curtiss told a *Post Dispatch* reporter, "Robinson is careful, skilled, a good mechanic and a great gentleman. He is conservative, yet he is daring enough to make excellent flights and please the spectators with some of the thrills. He has made many good flights."

When Robinson arrived in St. Louis, he was warmly received by his old friends who recalled the days of 1909, when he had attempted to fly his monoplane. Now he was in St. Louis as an exhibition flier and a celebrated guest of the St. Louis Aero Club at its headquarters at Kinloch Field. Aviation was progressing rapidly. Civic leaders joined aeronautical clubs, air fields were being built, and fliers had earned their wings. Robinson had flown scores of flights, some experimental, some exhibitional, and it was now in St. Louis that he finally earned his pilot's license.

Before the exhibition began, Tom Benoist asked Robinson to test fly his new biplane, the Benoist 8. Benoist had pretested the plane, but now Robinson was to put it through its paces, flying two straightaways, a figure eight, and the complete two-mile circumference of the field at a height of a hundred feet. With Benoist along on the wing, this was the first passenger-carrying flight to take place in St. Louis.

On June 11 Robinson flew his airplane five miles from Kinloch Field to the Glenn Echo Country Club. As anxious golfers watched, Robinson landed on the grounds, rolling into a tent in front of the clubhouse to avoid hitting a hedge (fig. 46). A broken spar was quickly repaired so Robinson could return to Kinloch Field.

46. *Following the landing mishap, a happy and relieved Robinson greets A. B. Lambert at Glen Echo Country Club.*

Preparations for the St. Louis air show included scheduling streetcars for special trips to Kinloch Field at a cost of ten cents per person. The admission fee was twenty-five cents. Most people could afford to attend this exciting event, and entire families were on hand to see the newest airplanes and watch the pilots fly.

A. B. Lambert and Hugh Robinson arranged to obtain Robinson's long-awaited pilot's license. Lambert was a well-known industrialist and city councilman who was president of the St. Louis Aero Club. Pilot licensing was being handled by the Aero Club of America, which authorized Lambert to supervise Robinson's test. The test requirements, as published by the organization, were as follows:

(A) Two distance tests, each consisting in covering, without touching the ground, a closed circuit not less than five kilometers in length (length measured as indicated below).

(B) An altitude test consisting in rising to a minimum height of 50 meters above the starting point.

(C) The (B) test may be made at the same time as one of the (A) tests.

The course over which the aviator shall accomplish the aforesaid two circuits must be indicated by two posts situated not more than 500 meters from each other.

After each turn made around a post the aviator will change his direction so as to leave the other post on his other side. The circuit will thus consist of an uninterrupted series of figure eights, each circle of the figure alternately encircling one of the posts. The distance credited over the course covered between two turns shall be the distance separating the two posts.

For each of these three tests the landing shall be made:

(1) By stopping the motor not later than the time when the machine touches the ground.

(2) At a distance of less than 50 meters from a point designated by the applicant before the test. Landings must be made properly and the official observer shall indicate in his report the way in which they were made, the issue of the license being always discretionary.

Rain prevented Robinson from flying for his license on the first appointed test day. The next day, despite winds of twenty miles per hour, Robinson flew successfully and was granted the forty-second pilots' license issued in this country (fig. 47).

At the St. Louis meet Robinson encountered high winds that prevented the scheduled display of cross-country flying, speed events, bomb-tossing, and taking two actresses aloft who had posed by Robinson's airplane. On the final day of the meet, Robinson presented an impressive display of his flying skills without incident. Performing with him were Tom Benoist and his ten aviation students, among whom was Enid Hibber, St. Louis' only aviatrix. The spectators were wildly enthusiastic.

Robinson was accompanied on one of his flights by Cagy Griffin, a journalist with the *St. Louis Star,* who described the flight on June 23 as "something different" and an experience he would not forget. Robinson had nonchalantly handed the writer a slip of paper to sign that released

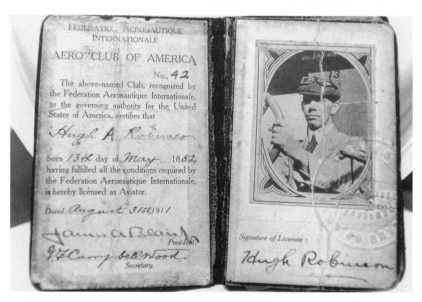

47. Robinson was awarded U.S. pilot's license number 42.

the Curtiss Exhibition Company from any and all responsibility in the event of damages or other legal action. When Griffin expressed surprise over the fact that Robinson had made no last-minute inspection of the airplane, Robinson replied that his machine was always in good order. He added that he would not promise barrel rolls or high speeds. These comments were the usual patronizing patter of a stunt pilot confronting his awed passenger.

Griffin rode on the board seat that rested on the lower wing back to the left of the pilot. He had to creep through a network of brace wires to reach the board, which was surrounded by wires and struts. Even though he was not tied in, Griffin felt relieved that it seemed impossible to fall out at any angle. When Robinson's assistants released the airplane and the aircraft began to move forward of its own volition, Griffin was struck by the plane's acceleration, which he likened to the "get away" of an athlete running in a sprint. When the weight began to lift from the wheels and the plane became magically airborne, the "sensation" began. The inspired reporter continued to describe the feeling as

> different from anything I had expected. It is not primarily a sensation of speed. I have seemed to go faster in an automobile, and probably have. It was not a sensation of billowy, gliding effort, as it looks from the ground: but, on the contrary, a rider feels a sense of irresistible power and life which is far apart from comfort.
>
> The sensation of flying more nearly resembles that of riding the cowcatcher of a speeding locomotive. You feel the throb and push of a great force behind you. You are at once trustful of that force to carry you safely, and yet feel an awe of its power. If a swift locomotive, shooting through the night had no headlight so that from the cowcatcher you need not see the ground, but could feel apart from the earth, you would have, I think, the sensation of flying.

Asked by the same reporter if he planned to follow in his famous father's footsteps, Hugh Robinson Jr. replied, "I'm not going to fly. I'm going to live as long as I can."

In rural communities of America, the Fourth of July was always an important occasion. The pilots would invariably pack the exhibition schedule for this day with as many events as possible, and the show usually ended with fireworks. On the nation's 135th birthday, the Curtiss show was in Cairo, Illinois, where the occasion was to be celebrated with an auto parade and a spectacular flying presentation featuring Robinson.

The Curtiss pusher had been removed from its piano crate atop a flatcar in the nearby railroad yard and taken to the aviation field. Spectators came from everywhere; several mountaineers arrived by oxcart. Many of the twenty-five thousand people in the crowd had never seen an airplane. There were so many visitors from out of town that Cairo's hotels issued a plea for help, and local residents were asked to leave their names at the Star Clothing Company if they had extra rooms they were willing to rent.

Cairo was at the juncture of three states: Illinois, Kentucky, and Missouri. There were also two rivers, the Ohio and the Mississippi, and three counties: Alexander, Mississippi, and Ballard. Robinson probably set a record by flying over all of the states, rivers, and counties. He also took a historic aerial photo of downtown Cairo, a bird's-eye view of the intersection of Eighth and Commercial streets, which showed an arch, an automobile driving along Commercial, and a number of pedestrians turning their heads to see the aviator and his plane. Robinson held his camera in his hand to take several such photos during his flight, a remarkable feat to perform while manually operating the controls of the fast-flying pusher airplane.

The *Daily Messenger* of Mayfield, Kentucky, describing the flights of the day in the hyperbole typical of journalism at that time, when newspapers competed for readership as well as promotion of major events, reported that "the aeroplane looked like a beautiful big dragon fly and the singing of the great and powerful motor was like the humming of the wings of a dragon fly with the combined brains of brainy men and with the confidence that comes of absolute fearlessness and mastery of the laws of the air."

According to the account in the *Cairo Citizen* on July 5, "So many people came that nearly all of Wickliffe, Bird's Point, plus the farmers of the adjacent county were transported to Cairo by the ferry boat 'Three States.' Professor Deal's 16 piece band played at different points in the business section during the day of the Fourth of July and at the bandstand in the afternoon and at the amphitheater during the fireworks display."

It was not known whether the fireworks display was actually "the greatest ever shown" or had actually been abbreviated because of the "tremendous cost of bringing in the air show and the new flying machine." It was rumored, however, that the fireworks committee was satisfied, confident that Cairo's population was pleased with the day's events.

Three unnamed but "fine musicians from St. Louis" were on hand to perform on this memorable Fourth of July. The local stores had closed early to allow their proprietors and clerks to witness "one of the most marvelous feats of the times," a tribute to Robinson's performance. Special steamboat excursions from as far away as Cape Girardeau were made to the river's harbor, carrying passengers who also came to see the flights and fireworks.

Midway through the festive weekend, Hugh Robinson came close to being killed when he flew the Curtiss pusher beneath a steel railroad bridge. The bridge's height was only seventy-five feet above water, and as Robinson was flying at a speed of sixty miles per hour, his plane was caught in a sudden gust of wind and nearly taken into one of the concrete support piers (fig. 48). The *Cairo Citizen* reported the near mishap as follows:

> When aviator Robinson made his last flight, he had a narrow escape from dashing to death against the Illinois Central Bridge. His flights were from the same grounds and in the same direction. The machine is generally made to rise against the wind, but the inadequate field facilities made it necessary for him to rise with the wind on both flights. In making his second flight, he headed the machine low between the Cairo Water Company's stand pipe and the Illinois Central Bridge. When he was about over the river, a treacherous wind caught the machine and carried it to

within less than five feet of the bridge. Mr. Robinson said that he was about to drop the machine to the river when he succeeded in turning safely from the steel structure. This was the second narrowest escape he has had since he has been a bird man.

Robinson's most dangerous mishap was his crash in Washington, D.C., when he flew into the mud yet was able to walk away.

Robinson described the flight that almost ended under the bridge as the most terrifying experience of his life. He was grateful that this had been the last flight of the day and that he would not have to take off downwind across the river again. It had been a most dangerous maneuver because the lift beneath the wings is lowered as the flow of wind is diminished. Flying into the wind gives a plane more lift and fewer downdrafts. Now he knew that large stationary objects could alter the wind in many dangerous ways. He had also gained respect for the dangers of taking off downwind, which was often necessary.

The man who almost always flew with his lucky 13 painted on his radiator saw good fortune once again in a career marked by relatively few mishaps compared to those of so many of his fellow pilots whose lives had ended prematurely.

48. Robinson was flying under the Illinois Central Bridge at Cairo when a gust of wind almost tossed him into the support structure.

C H A P T E R 6

Hydroplane and Pusher Exhibition, 1911–1912

Immediately following the Cairo exhibition, Robinson joined Glenn Curtiss at Hammondsport, New York, where he continued work on improving the hydroplane. The men ran numerous tests on Lake Keuka, and eventually Robinson flew the hydroplane, with its seventy-five-horsepower engine, seventy-four miles per hour over the water, a new speed record for such water craft. Reporters had become entranced by the hydro, which was not an airship or a motorboat or an automobile but a combination of all three. One reporter enthusiastically named the hydro "a spider, a bat and a fast motorboat with wings." Whatever it was called, the hydro was fast, skimming over boats in the harbor. This was one of the fliers' favorite tricks, and it often caused confusion and concern to startled boaters.

Of flying at Hammondsport, Robinson wrote, "The general impression among aviators and manufacturers of aeroplanes is that the hydroplane is rapidly becoming the flying craft of the future by reason of its ease of control, extensive bodies of water upon which to operate it, and above all, its safety."

In the *Curtiss Aviation Book*, which was published to promote Curtiss-built planes, Robinson noted, "It is practically impossible for the operator of a hydroaeroplane to suffer injury in the event of an accident. Even in the worst kind of accident, the most that can happen to the operator is an exhilarating plunge into salt or fresh water, as the case may be, with the beneficial effects of a good swim if so desired. Otherwise, the operator may 'stand by' the wreckage which cannot possibly sink."

The hydroplane had many positive characteristics. Robinson believed it was safe because of the friction between the float and water on takeoff. This plane also required greater power than a land plane, offering safer turning or climbing at takeoff. The Curtiss hydro pontoon had six separate compartments so that it could not sink even if part of the pontoon were to be severely damaged in an accident. Robinson stated in an article that, in a test, "two compartments were filled with water on purpose by pulling a drain plug, and the hydro took off without the slightest difficulty."

The hydro could be operated on waves six to eight feet in height and could land in crosswinds. This was because the plane's design allowed for a certain slip on the water, which would be devastating to any land plane. Also, when the hydro made its water run hitting thirty-five miles per hour, it skimmed over the surface, then broke free into the air. Many writers called this action "jumping" in their descriptions of the "spider-like thing with the roaring noise."

Curtiss and his team spent a long time perfecting the hydro in preparation for marketing it in Europe and Russia. The Russian Aerial League displayed interest in ordering one of the hydroplanes. The French were most intrigued by the single-pontoon Curtiss aircraft, since most European hydroplanes, much like catamarans, bore twin pontoons, which frequently disintegrated on high seas.

Among Robinson's tasks at that time was writing several chapters on the hydroplane for the *Curtiss Aviation Book*. He wrote about the operation of the plane in some detail:

> The operation of a hydro is very similar to that of the ordinary land machine . . . only if anything, considerably easier and more simple. The start of the hydro is simply starting the motor while the hydro is resting on the land or bank of the lake or river, with the front towards the water.

The operator takes his place, and on opening the throttle gradually the thrust of the motor slides the apparatus along the ground, or planks if ground be unsuitable, and into the water. The pontoon, being fitted underneath with steel shod runners made it possible to start on rocks, gravel, or, in fact, most any reasonable surface. The finish can be made in the same manner, without assistance.

It is possible to start the hydro on dry land if the surface is reasonably smooth, with the assistance of one or two mechanics. It is also possible, in an emergency, even to land on the earth with the hydro pontoon attachment and of course, with wheels attached to the landing gear, one can come down on land as with the ordinary type of machine. Once out on the open water, the operator rapidly increases his speed by opening the throttle, taking care, however, to accelerate gradually, to allow the pontoon to mount the surface of the water without throwing an unnecessary amount of water into the propeller.

Once a speed of twenty-five miles to thirty miles an hour is obtained, the pontoon skims lightly over the surface of the water. As the ailerons do not become effective until the machine acquires considerable speed, the small floats on the lower ends of the wings maintain the balance until necessary speed is acquired.

When the machine has acquired a certain speed it leaves the water in exactly the same manner as on the land and immediately increases its speed, due to the released friction from the water. It also has a slight tendency to jump into the air due to this released friction. . . . Once into the air, the operation is the same as with the regular land-equipped Curtiss aeroplanes.

The landing is made in the same manner, bearing in mind to keep the boat as near level fore and aft as possible, and if the water be very rough to allow the tail of the machine to settle on the water first. This will prevent any possibility of sticking the front of the boat into an unexpected wave. As should be the case with any aeroplane, it is advisable to start and land against the wind if there be much, but this is not compulsory. The hydro may be landed even while drifting sideways, in an emergency case. It is obvious that to do this with a land machine would be to invite disaster.

During this period in Hammondsport, Curtiss was grooming Robinson to be his first and top hydroplane pilot as part of the Curtiss Exhibition Team. Robinson became familiar with all of the modifications as they evolved. While his own hydroplane was being prepared, Robinson was asked to perform in his Curtiss pusher once again at Rochester, New York.

On July 13, Robinson, Lincoln Beachy, and Beckwith Havens arrived at the aviation field in Rochester (fig. 49). The three-day program there included twelve events; speed flights, altitude flights, bomb-dropping, slow flying, head-on flying, and short-start competitive flights.

"Both Robinson and Beachy had their biplanes under great control," said a local press account of the occasion. "They did figure eights, circles and all kinds of foolhardy stunts." "Beachy and Robinson Flirt with Death," ran the headline. They both had indeed come close to death. Robinson had prearranged with Beachy that Beachy should do a stunt dive under his machine. Robinson heard Beachy's motor behind him and erroneously concluded that Beachy was above him. Robinson began dropping to get out of Beachy's way. A moment later, Beachy had to swerve out from under Robinson's falling craft, missing Robinson's landing gear by only three or four feet. The wash of air from Beachy's machine sent Robinson dropping like a shot for two hundred feet. He regained control of the plane when it was only twenty-five feet above a clump of trees.

Lincoln Beachy was considered one of the most daring stunt pilots of his time. Robinson was proud of the fact that he had given this star some of his earliest flying lessons. He was a fearless aviator who defied death without flinching as the crowds demanded more and more excitement. He would go into a steep dive until the wires whined and the plane was at its limit, then come out of the dive moments before hitting the ground. Beachy also held the record for fast climbing by rising 6,500 feet in fifteen minutes. On another day he put only ten gallons of gas in his tank and, with just a small saddle seat between him and the ground below, flew straight upward, breaking the world altitude record of 11,642 feet. Upon reaching this altitude, he had used all of his fuel and had to glide his

OFFICIAL PROGRAM

ROCHESTER AVIATION MEET

Under the auspices of the

ROCHESTER HERALD

AT THE

ROCHESTER AVIATION FIELD

——•——

JULY 13th, 14th, 15th, 1911

PROGRAM OF EVENTS

NOTICE: The events listed in this program are subject to change or cancellation on account of autmospheric conditions, accidents, or other unavoidable causes.

The order in which events will be carried out will be indicted by numbered cards posted on the announcement board. The NUMBER on the bulletin board indicates the EVENT as listed in this Program; the LETTER posted with the number indicates the AVIATOR or AVIATORS participating in that particular event.

AVIATORS' LETTERS

LINCOLN BEACHEY **[A]**

HUGH A. ROBINSON **[B]**   BECKWITH HAVENS **[C]**

NUMBER OF EVENTS

EVENT No. 1—SPEED COMPETITION; daily, five miles.
EVENT No. 2—ALTITUDE COMPETITION.
EVENT No. 3—SPEED COMPETITION; three miles.
EVENT No. 4—BOMB DROPPING COMPETITION; hitting battleship target on ground greatest number of times during meet.
EVENT No. 5—MATCH RACE FROM SCRATCH, one mile.
EVENT No. 6—SPEED COMPETITION WITH PASSENGER.
EVENT No. 7—QUICK CLIMBING COMPETITION; to 1000 feet altitude.
EVENT No. 8—SHORT STARTING COMPETITION.
EVENT No. 9—ACCURATE FLYING COMPETITION; starting ane alighting in one hundred foot circle.
EVENT No. 10—MILITARY EXPERIMENTS; sharpshooting, etc.
EVENT No. 11—EXHIBITION FLIGHT; introducing spiral glide, circle dip, volplaning, etc
EVENT No. 12—SLOW FLYING COMPETITION; five laps of track.

Extra Events not included in the Program will be announced.

49. An advertisement for an early air meet featuring Hugh Robinson, Lincoln Beachy, and Beckwith Havens at Rochester, New York. The ad shows the type of flying events they conducted, which ranged from speed competition to dive-bombing.

airplane back to the ground. He was the first pilot to fly upside down without crashing and the third man in the world to loop-the-loop.

From July 20 to July 22, Robinson and Ely flew exhibitions at Seattle, Washington. "Thousands watch manbirds in flight over city and bay," the headlines ran across the front page of the Seattle paper. Ely flew the Curtiss pusher, and Robinson was in the hydroplane for the first time as a member of the Curtiss Exhibition Team. The newspapers were elated to have this news to report. "It is simply a fast motorboat with wings that fly like a great silk-winged bat," they stated. It must be noted that journalists were more and more frequently searching for new metaphors in which to describe the experience of flying. In an article in a Seattle paper, the hydro was likened to "a bat . . . a spider . . . a beetle." The article also stated that Ely was "soaring hawklike" and Robinson was "soaring like a gull." In describing the airplane, a writer used the term "big fish." After one flight, an article stated that "the great machine lay there at the end, panting."

While Ely was "strolling through elysian fields of the upper ether" in the pusher, Robinson was delighting the spectators with his "swim-flight" over Seattle's busy harbor. "A great splash of foam and spray and the little black spider-thing was shooting in a straight line for the cluster of gunboats anchored about a mile away," the newspaper reported. And "for fully a half-mile the machine sped along at a rate of 50 miles an hour, then the man in the seat laid a light finger on the control lever . . . and the beetle sprang into the air 500 feet. Ely circled above, Hawklike, and at 200 feet he concluded the show by crossing in front of the crowd amid the deafening din of wild hand-clapping, shrieks and cheering."

"I was flying at 65 miles an hour while in the air," Robinson told a dazed newsman. "The machine will not leave the water at a speed of less than 50 miles an hour. I know that it is hard to realize the speed by watching from a distance. I know that it is heavy, the pontoon alone weighs 75 pounds but was reduced from 150 pounds with our work at Hammondsport. I was mostly flying at 100 feet and did not attempt to go high. The waves on landing gave me no trouble. I crossed the swells of a number of vessels and jumped from one wave top to another without trouble. The only drawback is the spray which hits me."

In July, Robinson presented an excellent performance before thousands of spectators in Vincennes, Indiana. His Curtiss pusher had never been in better shape. Robinson demonstrated good judgment by waiting for the calm of evening before attempting to fly his machine. This was difficult because there were thousands of eager spectators waiting impatiently, irritated by the heat and the seemingly interminable delays between events.

Once he was in the air, however, Robinson so thrilled the throngs with his stunts that they soon forgot their frustration. Watching a race between an automobile and an airplane was always a favorite with viewers. It was in a race of this kind that Robinson performed at his best in Vincennes—and won.

In August, Robinson participated in the Gimbels Brothers Race in New York City, which was the heavyweight championship of aviation. Glenn Curtiss had sent three of his most popular pilots to fly in the race, which was important in promoting the airplanes that bore his name. This was a day of intense competition as Curtiss sought to achieve victories and set new records to further his own name as well as increase sales.

Hugh Robinson, Lincoln Beachy, and Charles Hamilton were selected to fly in the overland event from New York to Philadelphia. This was the first American cross-country race, an important event for all who were anxious to see who would fly from city to city to win the five thousand dollars in prize money that had been put up by Gimbel Brothers Department Stores of New York and Philadelphia. This was a large prize for a single pilot to win. The aviators were to take off from Governors Island in New York Harbor and then fly up the Hudson River and on to the Gimbel building at Broadway and Thirty-third Street, the official starting point. To demonstrate the potential of flight for mail delivery, each of the contestants was to carry bags filled with messages and packages. These were to be dropped off over towns along their route. Among the well-known spectators on the roof at Gimbels was Orville Wright. Also present were other members of the New York Aero Club, which was timing the event at the starting point.

The route the men took to Philadelphia followed the Pennsylvania Railroad tracks as far as Trenton, New Jersey, then down the Delaware River to Market Street in Philadelphia, and up Market Street to the finish line above the Philadelphia Gimbels store. From there they flew up the Schuylkill River and landed at Fairmont Park. All in all, the course covered 130 miles. No aviation chart was available to the pilots; their only instrument was a wristwatch. The daring Lincoln Beachy won the contest in a brilliant flight that ended with a spiral dip over the statue of William Penn at City Hall before he landed.

Before reaching Philadelphia, Robinson had become lost while attempting to follow the railroad ties from the air. He had also confused New Brunswick with Trenton when he stopped to refuel. Although he had exerted a great deal of effort to catch up with the others, the winds were not in his favor. It is reported that Beachy had also become lost briefly but had recovered with no difficulty. Ely had had to stop midway for gas tank repairs and eventually abandoned the race altogether.

Following the Gimbels race, Robinson took his hydroplane to Chicago for his next event. It was a well-attended meet that took place on the lakefront at Grant Park. Robinson was the only pilot entered with a hydroplane, since no other reliable hydroplane existed in the United States. He made daily flights from both land and water. Robinson's skill with this craft attracted much attention as he flew out over the lake and back over the park, circling boats and landing next to them. Before massive crowds, for the first time, he demonstrated the safety and versatility of water flying.

It was during this meet that the first water rescue was made by a plane of any kind (fig. 50). Two nonamphibious airplanes fell into Lake Michigan, and Robinson attempted to rescue the pilots in his hydroplane. One of the airmen, St. Croix Johnstone, had "dropped from the clouds and was drowned a mile offshore of Chicago Beach." A local newspaper stated,

> No sooner had the aviator flying the Curtiss hydroaeroplane noticed the accident when he immediately launched his airship and set out to the point where Johnstone had disappeared beneath the surface of Lake Michigan. Around this point he circled time after time vainly waiting for the aviator to come to the surface. Had the aviator appeared there is no ques-

tion but that by means of the hydroaeroplane a life would have been saved from drowning. This is the first time on record in the world's history that an aircraft of any kind has been utilized to save anyone from drowning.

A happier part of the story was told in the following account, published subsequently in another local paper:

Life saving in time of peace, while it has not attained more than a fraction of the number of lives saved in war is perhaps more interesting to most people than the latter, being closer to daily needs and experiences of the general public. It is therefore gratifying to find that the water aeroplane, the hydroaeroplane and the flying boat seem destined to save lives. The hydroaeroplane demonstrated its efficiency as a life saver in 1911, while still in the experimental period. It was during the famous Chicago meet that an aviator lost control while flying over Lake Michigan and fell into the water. Three-quarters of a mile away there was a hydroaeroplane, the early Curtiss model . . . the prototype of the flying boat . . . circling around and occasionally setting on the surface of the

50. Wreckage from the Johnstone airplane that crashed into Lake Michigan during the August 1911 air show being towed ashore. Robinson flew out in the hydroplane to attempt to rescue Johnstone, but he had already drowned. This was the first sea rescue attempt by plane.

water like a big sea gull. The pilot of this craft, seeing the aviator fall, went to the rescue. Flying at a mile a minute speed, he reached the spot, landed on the water by the submerged aeroplane and offered to take the aviator to land—all in less than one minute.

The survivor was the famed French aviator René Simon (fig. 51).

Following a one-day exhibition at Manola Lake, Indiana, after the Chicago meet, Robinson proceeded to Astoria, Oregon, to make the first flight from the Columbia River. The huge crowd assembled there included government officials. Robinson's first flight went smoothly. On his second flight, however, he unexpectedly hit a large wave, and the propeller, both wings, and the pontoon were splintered. The hydroplane flipped on its back in the water, and all that could be seen was Robinson squatting on the upturned pontoon, gesturing to the anxious crowd that he was fine (fig. 52). He was the first to claim a belly-up crash landing on the famous Western river. Robinson drifted downstream, calmly clinging to the pontoon while directing the salvage operation. Despite this mishap, the show was a splendid success. Three women, believing the aviator had been killed in the accident, fainted in the stands.

51. *The third pilot who crashed into Lake Michigan was the famous French pilot René Simon. Robinson reached him in a matter of minutes in his hydro.*

52. *The wrecked hydro was upside down in the water with Robinson squatting on the bottom of the pontoon.*

Because of a ruined magneto, the hydro could not be repaired. Robinson frantically attempted to locate and order a replacement magneto from Hammondsport so that he could meet future contracts. This would have taken a great deal of time, however, since transportation was slow and magnetos were scarce. At the next exhibition, in Glenwood Springs, Colorado, Robinson had to fly the pusher instead of the hydro.

While he was in Glenwood Springs, Robinson encountered a phenomenon previously undiscovered in aviation—true rarified air. Flying at higher altitudes was a new experience. On the second day of the exhibition, while attempting to take off, Robinson was thrown from his craft after flying through telephone wires and a picket fence. No one knew that an aircraft's ability to climb would be reduced in high altitudes, where the air was not so dense as it was at sea level. Becoming airborne in thinner air required greater speed and a longer runway. Fortunately, Robinson was not badly hurt, and he calmly walked over to his damaged aircraft and turned off the engine. We now know why the pilots of early aircraft did not wear seat belts: they preferred the possibility of being thrown from the aircraft "on their feet" to being strapped to the board seat in the front of the craft in the event of a crash.

In early September, Robinson appeared in Amarillo, Texas. After the air show there his airplane was dismantled and shipped to Clay Center, Kansas, for a flight on September 8. Strong, gusting winds, however, prevented all flying that day. The spectators at the Norton County fair were disappointed but accepted the fact that pilot safety came first. Unfortunately, the Curtiss Exhibition Team was paid only when it performed.

On September 12 Robinson was scheduled to perform with Cromwell Dixon, but Dixon was unable to fly because he had been injured during an exhibition at Marshalltown, Iowa. Robinson had known Dixon as a balloonist in St. Louis, where he had devised a cigar-shaped balloon, powered by a small propeller and operated with bicycle pedals. Dixon had been only fourteen at the time and had been known as the youngest aviator in the world. Five years later he earned ten thousand dollars by becoming the first aviator to fly over the Rocky Mountains. His career ended a week after this spectacular flight when he was killed at the age of nineteen during a performance in Spokane, Washington.

While in Williston, North Dakota, that September, Robinson wrote an article for the *Williston Daily News,* published on September 17, 1911, describing the plans he had with Glenn Curtiss to fly across the Atlantic Ocean in a hydro:

> How I shall fly across the ocean in my sea-going flying machine?
>
> Somebody has to be the first to fly across the Atlantic. For it goes without saying that it will be done sooner or later. I think it will be done soon rather than later, and I want to be the man to blaze the way.
>
> I believe that this thing of flying across the Atlantic is now a mere matter of arranging the details. We have aeroplanes that will fly as long as their fuel holds out, and the Curtiss hydroaeroplane that can skim the waves like a petrel. Flying across the ocean, then, becomes merely a matter of building a machine that can carry enough fuel to drive it across, or of distributing a series of supply ships along the route to be covered.

Personally, I think that the cross-ocean flight will first be accomplished by the latter expedient: that a hydroaeroplane, perhaps somewhat more powerful than those now in use, will make the trip by flying from one to another of a number of 'nurse ships.' Thus, one man might make the trip by resting between flights on-board the nurse ships, or the machine could be sent through without delay, by relays of aviators with each man covering one stage.

Crossing thus, by stages, with periods of rest between, will be a flight interrupted only for taking on fuel. I won't say that it will never be done in one flight without pause, but for the present, the question of fuel makes that out of the question. No aeroplane of the present type can carry enough fuel, such as is now used, to carry it 3,000 miles. But a hydroaeroplane of the present type, with a sufficiently strong and reliable motor, might do it by taking on fuel at sea. It would need to be equipped to carry a crew of at least two men, however, each a pilot so that there could be rotation in control to give the aviators time to rest. For, at best, it would take twenty or twenty-four hours to make the trip.

There isn't as much danger attached to an ocean flight as one would naturally expect. If the very worst comes and you have to take to the water, the hydroaeroplane will bear you up almost indefinitely. For it rides the waves like a duck. It is emphatically a good sea boat. It doesn't feel the shock of the waves as an ordinary boat does, but bobs from crest to crest like a cork. I would trust the hydroaeroplane to outride a fairly heavy blow.

As to the route to be chosen, that would probably be decided by weather conditions. Of course, the shortest passage would be from Nova Scotia to Ireland, but to cover that route would necessitate flying over the iceberg-infested North Atlantic and across the foggy stretch of the sea east of the Canadian seaboard. So it's likely that the first crossing will cover a longer and more temperate route, perhaps following the Gulf Stream from New York, or Boston, to England.

Anyhow, I am convinced that the transatlantic flight can be accomplished, and I am looking forward to the time, not far distant I hope, when I can have a try at it.

Hugh Robinson never made the transatlantic flight. It was not until
May 1919 that U.S. Navy Lt. Comdr. Albert C. Read and his crew flew the
first transatlantic flight, in a Curtiss NC-4 seaplane, from Rockaway, Long
Island, to Plymouth, England. The flight lasted fifty-two hours and thirty-
one minutes, making stops at Newfoundland, the Azores, and Portugal.

By the end of 1911, the impatient air show crowds wanted even more
excitement for their money. When weather permitted, Robinson gave the
people the thrills they sought, but his stunts were never as daring as those
performed by the other Curtiss team members.

William J. "Shack" Shackelford was Curtiss's mechanic in Hammondsport and North Island and was also present on the Exhibition Team's
tour. While Fanciulli had worked ahead of the team to make bookings,
sign contracts, and arrange for promotion, Shack stayed with Robinson to
keep him flying. The boyish-looking blond mechanic supervised the repairs and maintenance of Robinson's airplanes and the hand-propping of
the machines for a salary of about twenty-five dollars a week. Robinson
knew that his success and safety depended on this mechanic, who was
highly skilled, although painstakingly slow and compulsive about mechanical details.

"An aeroplane is something like an automobile when it comes to starting it," declared the *Mansfield Tribune* of October 11, 1911. "The propeller
is started much like a huge auto 'crank' is manipulated; only it takes the
whole weight of the body and all the strength of the muscles to pull it
through. . . . If Shack weren't pretty nimble and allowed himself to get in
the way of one of the blades, he would instantly be cut in two by the
knife-like shaft."

If he had not spent the whole night tending to the planes, Shackelford
could be seen back at work in the early hours, oiling the valves, polishing
the spark plugs, directing his assistants in the work of binding poles with
fine wire or patching any tiny rips in the wings of the craft, or telling the
other mechanics to give him a boost as he inspected the planes. Shackelford

53. With the hydro out of commission, Robinson joined Jimmy Ward in Sedalia, Missouri. The men are shown trying to outrun a race car.

would assemble the entire aircraft before each exhibition and disassemble and crate it afterward for the journey by train to the next town.

Robinson and Shack continued their travels through the Midwest in September and early October, stopping at towns along the railroad route that provided transportation on flatcars or in covered boxcars for the crated aircraft. Robinson performed in Huron, South Dakota; McAlaster, Oklahoma; Chanute, Kansas; Dubuque, Iowa; Houghton Lake, Michigan; Evansville, Indiana; Sedalia, Missouri (fig. 53); Muskogee, Oklahoma; and St. Louis.

In McAlaster, Robinson flew over the state prison at the request of the warden so that the prisoners could see an airplane fly. Many of the inmates had been incarcerated before the invention of the airplane in 1903, and some might have died in prison without ever having seen a flight. The prisoners were jubilant as they gathered in the yard to see Robinson fly his hydroplane.

In Evansville the airplane was used in another new technology—the newsreel. A photographer from Pathé News was on hand to record Robinson's flights for the company's weekly newsreel review of international current events. This provided a unique opportunity for Evansville to become better known to the rest of the world.

On his return to St. Louis in October 1911 with his rebuilt hydroplane, Robinson made local history during an exhibition flight, becoming the first aeronaut to take off from the Mississippi River. He also raced motorboats, flew under bridges, delivered the mail (fig. 54), and made diving runs in front of the spectators gathered on the riverfront, who were extremely proud of their homegrown aviator (fig. 55).

By performing in the 1911 St. Louis World's Fair and Exposition, Robinson was able to prepare for the upcoming flight he planned to make down the Mississippi River. He had been tempted by a purse of twenty thousand dollars as well as another ten thousand dollars that cities along

54. Robinson accepts a sack of mail for delivery by air.

55. Robinson being towed to shore at the St. Louis Centennial exhibition flight. The importance of the wingtip floats is apparent.

the route had raised for the first pilot to fly from Minnesota to Louisiana along the broad and sluggish river.

Meanwhile, a pilot by the name of C. P. Rodgers was flying from New York to California and had already covered 1,398 miles in his Wright pusher. The Mississippi flight would be a distance of 1,917 miles, and Robinson had devised a plan to make it America's first airmail flight. He had scheduled stops in many cities, and he knew large crowds would gather along the way to see him land and take off. The postmaster general of the United States authorized Robinson to carry mail sacks on the flight to be dropped off en route.

When the time came for the flight, Robinson attempted for three consecutive days to take off from Lake Calhoun, a wide body of water in a residential area of Minneapolis. Local postmaster W. D. Hale, who had handed Robinson a sack of mail for the flight, looked on with dismay as the plane struggled unsuccessfully to become airborne on a hot, still day. Large crowds returned day after day to witness the start down the Mississippi, never losing interest as the plane taxied back and forth to no avail.

On October 17 a sudden gust of wind of the kind sometimes called a dust devil bore down onto the calm lake and forced Robinson back into the water during takeoff, damaging the pontoon. The pontoon was replaced, and the mail pack was reduced in weight from fifty to twenty-five pounds to lighten the load. Robinson was then finally able to take off, clearing a high, wide bridge by only a few feet. The long water run lay ahead, and his spectators watched and waited.

Robinson's next stop was Red Wing, Minnesota. As he flew at a thousand feet with poor visibility and in turbulent winds, he noted that he was running low on fuel. His watch indicated that he was near Red Wing, so he descended to eight hundred feet, finding that he was over Lake Pepin, far past Red Wing (fig. 56). The wings rocked violently, and suddenly the right wing shot down as the nose tilted toward the ground. Robinson twisted and pulled at the controls to no avail. The plane was in the grip of a corkscrew turn, later termed a tailspin. Robinson crawled out onto the pontoon, and, holding on to the bamboo outrigger with one hand and the steering wheel with the other, he prepared to jump into the water below. He later explained: "As I got lower I inched farther out on the high side of the pontoon and when I was less than 100 feet from the water the plane slowly straightened out into level flight. I crawled back into the seat and grabbed the controls. My weight on the high side of the plane counteracted the revolving motion the same as a rudder does today and it saved my life."

Pilots have since learned that they can pull out of a tailspin following a stall by applying the rudder opposite the direction of the spin and lowering the nose. The added speed and the opposite rudder stop the corkscrew turning of the plane, and the controls can then be pulled back to level the nose and allow the plane to continue on a straight path.

About thirteen miles north of Winona, Minnesota, Robinson ran out of

56. *Robinson's first stop on the Mississippi flight was to be at Red Wing, Minnesota. Because of poor visibility, however, he overshot the city and landed on the river in Winona. Here he punctured his pontoon on a low, rocky dam and had to be towed ashore, where he was welcomed by a group of townspeople.*

gas and had to make a forced landing on the Mississippi River. Inadvertently, he hit a hidden dam and ripped a huge hole in his pontoon. Some local boaters towed him to the place where he was supposed to land in Winona, where thousands of people had been waiting. The next day Robinson learned that he had flown a hundred and ten miles in eighty-nine minutes—a world speed record of eighty-one miles an hour, made possible by the strong tailwind. In the process, he had bypassed Red Wing.

It took two days to repair the pontoon so that Robinson could set out again. On the next leg of his trip, to La Crosse, Wisconsin, he almost ran into a launch as he was taking off downwind from Winona. He was able to lift off the water, but because he was unable to clear the two bridges in his path, he had to fly under them. He turned the hydro to head back into the wind in order to gain altitude, but again he could not clear the bridges.

Once more he had to fly underneath them. On October 19 Robinson flew to La Crosse, where he stopped to put on an exhibition to promote interest in overwater flying and to pick up and deliver mail. He refueled and then went on to Prairie du Chien, Wisconsin. While he was flying down the Mississippi at three thousand feet, a bolt fell out of the steering gear, making it impossible to control the rigging. At first Robinson did not know how he would be able to land the hydro, but he managed by leaning forward against the steering column and thus causing the plane to lose altitude gradually. He landed safely and was able to replace the bolt and continue the trip. New Orleans lay far in the distance. Agents in the towns ahead were frustrated as they tried to pacify the impatient crowds that appeared daily to see the pilot who seldom arrived on schedule.

Dubuque, Iowa, was to be an important stop for Robinson. At this point he had begun to glide down for a landing on the near side of two parallel bridges that spanned the river. As he neared the approach for a water landing, he noticed that the throngs awaited him on the far side of the bridges, which were very close together. Robinson hit the throttle, but, unable to clear the bridges, he flew under them instead. He later discovered that he had had only twenty feet of clearance between the water and the bridges. The spectators assumed that Robinson had put on a great stunt. In reality, it was an error in judgment made by the habitually cautious aviator.

After Robinson's arrival in Dubuque, he was told of Ely's death a few days earlier at the state fair in Macon, Georgia. Ely had failed to pull out of a dive. As he hit the ground, he was thrown out of his seat. The news seemed to crush Robinson's spirit—he had never been able to cope easily with the news of a flier friend's death. When approached by a reporter for his comments, he said, "Ely was one of the most careful operators I knew, and only an accident that was unforeseen could have caused this death." But Ely had pushed his luck too far. Later, on October 21, 1911, the *Moline Dispatch* reported Robinson's comments: "Ely was one of the most careful of the Curtiss clan of aviators, but during the last summer he has been associating considerably with Lincoln Beachy, and I believe the influence had some effect on him. For he has been practicing aerial gymnastics considerably. He was a fine young fellow and every one of us who knew him were greatly grieved at his loss."

Continuing on the Mississippi River flight, on October 20 Robinson flew from Dubuque to Bellevue and then to Clinton, Iowa, where he refueled. The next stop on the trip was Rock Island, Illinois. When Robinson landed, he learned that some of the towns ahead had begun to cancel their bookings. He also realized that it was late in the season and that further financial support would not be forthcoming from St. Louis. He therefore canceled the Mississippi flight while he was in Rock Island. The dream ended there, 375 miles from his start.

While Robinson had failed to set the long-distance record, his flight had other significance. Because of a tailwind, he had established a new speed record and made the longest overwater flight to that time. He had discovered a primitive form of spin recovery. He had also delivered mail by air to six cities, making the longest authorized mail flight to date. Several weeks earlier, Earl Ovington, generally known as the first United States airmail pilot, had become the first person to fly mail officially. He had taken his cargo from Nassau Boulevard Airdrome, Long Island, to Mineola, Long Island, a distance of six miles.

After his stressful flight down the Mississippi River, Robinson returned to his boyhood home in Neosho, where he spent ten days recovering with his wife, children, and mother. Then he went to Wichita for what would prove to be one of his last shows with the Curtiss Exhibition Team. Robinson was scheduled to continue on to Austin, Texas; Savannah, Georgia; Spartanburg, South Carolina; and then into Mexico before taking time off to winter in Cuba.

November 10 in Wichita marked the beginning of change. While Robinson was landing his biplane in the flat Kansas prairie, his wheel caught in a hole, and he was thrown from the plane with tremendous force. He heard the engine whistling over his head before it buried itself in the ground in a noisy crash landing. Robinson suffered a broken collar-bone, his third such injury in his years of flying.

Despite his misfortune, Robinson still considered flying to be safe. "All the aeroplane accidents which have resulted in deaths in this country have been the result of poor judgment or grandstand playing," he said. "Nearly all the boys who are flying in this country at the present time are merely kids and like to take a chance once in awhile. Even at that, there have been only about a hundred deaths in flying, while about a million flights have been made, which is a smaller percentage of fatalities than have resulted from automobile driving, street car operations, or travel on steam railroads."

CHAPTER 7

Hydroplane Flights on the French Riviera, 1912

Robinson had lost his enthusiasm for exhibition flying, traveling from city to city across America. He wanted to go back to experimental flying. His family was weary of living in railroad cars and hotels. The Robinsons chose therefore to move back to Hammondsport, New York.

As luck would have it, however, Robinson was soon flying exhibitions again, though for different reasons. Much time and money had been dedicated to the development of the safe and dependable hydroplane, and Glenn Curtiss now felt justified in saying that no one could match his progress. He proceeded with plans to set up a branch operation in Europe. At the same time, Louis Paulhan, the gallant and amicable French aviator who had won a prize of fifty thousand dollars for flying from London to Manchester in the exciting Farman plane, came to Hammondsport to see Curtiss. Paulhan was recognized as the great flyer who had flown the Bleriot monoplane in many European air exhibitions. He was so impressed with the American hydroplane and with Robinson's flying ability that he approached Curtiss about sending him and Robinson as agents to the French Riviera to convince the French military to buy American hydros. There were other developers of the hydroplane in Europe who used various types of pontoons. None, however, flew like the Curtiss hydro, especially when Robinson piloted it.

Curtiss agreed to have Paulhan act as his agent in France and to establish a flight training base at the Juan-les-Pins casino near Nice. Robinson was to teach Paulhan to fly, and the men would put on exhibitions for the French and other foreign governments, including Russia. They knew the French navy was holding military maneuvers close to the coast of France.

Robinson, Jerome Fanciulli (Curtiss's New York business representative), and mechanic W. J. "Shack" Shackelford sailed for Europe on the SS *Amerika* on January 9, 1912. This was to be Fanciulli's last year with Curtiss; after assisting in selling the hydro to France and Russia, he would be on his own. The aviators packed four unassembled hydros totaling forty thousand dollars in value in crates that were put into the hold of the *Amerika*. One of these was destined for sale to the Russians for their Aerial League at Sebastopol, on the Black Sea.

Robinson had been concentrating on an enormous publicity stunt that would tell the whole world he had arrived with his hydros. He planned to assemble a hydro on the top deck of the ship and have it lowered by a deck derrick onto the water while they were at sea in mid-winter. He had designed a ratchet and cable arrangement that would allow him to start the engine with the airplane in the water, since he would be unable to turn the propeller by hand and operate the controls at the same time. It was impossible to move about in a biplane at sea without becoming thoroughly soaked. The ratchet and cable hand pump was a significant invention before the advent of the electric self-starter.

Robinson had been forewarned by the ship's captain of the danger of being lost at sea because he had no instruments and could easily stray from his course. Robinson persisted, however, saying he was aware of the potential danger and that if someone on the liner would just point out the direction of Hamburg, Germany, and blow a whistle three times when Robinson was airborne, he could get on with his plan. Robinson also planned to carry and deliver the ship's mail, and he had been given a letter authorizing him to do so.

When the day of the event finally arrived, the ship came to a stop approximately twenty miles from shore. With passengers looking at Robinson aboard the hydro, the aircraft was lowered to the water, and the engine was started. It caught, and the propeller flashed. After Robinson signaled that he was ready, he cast off, taxiing out over a gray and wintery sea, skimming almost two miles across the top of huge swells. Robinson then circled the ship, and three whistle blasts sounded. As he ascended and headed toward the coast, the ship's captain muttered something about "lunatics."

The flight itself was not a problem until Robinson arrived at the mouth of the River Elbe, which was coated with a thin sheet of ice. Since Robinson was out of gas, he had to land the hydro on the frozen river. When he did so, there was a loud, splintering noise as the ice cracked and shattered like glass under the impact, and Robinson was hurled through the wings, which were completely shredded. The pontoon was also severely damaged. Only the watertight partitions that made up the pontoon prevented the plane from sinking. Robinson commented on the ice landing as follows:

> The next thing I saw when I came up from ducking the dangerous, needle-like ice, was a group of natives running across the river toward me. Their mouths were wide open and they stood around at a distance spellbound because they had never seen a plane before. They were busy jabbering in German and the only word I could catch was, "Amerika . . . Amerika". I wondered how they realized I had flown in from the S.S. "Amerika." Then I saw them pointing to two American Flags fitted to the struts on my wings.
>
> They thought I had flown to Hamburg from America!
>
> So did customs officials who secured the plane and took me down to the office. There I had to clear myself and assure them I had not crossed the ocean without a passport.

This was the beginning of Robinson's European adventure.

The remaining hydros arrived at Juan-les-Pins by rail. A small hangar was provided so that the planes could be safely stored and easily moved to

57. Hugh Robinson standing next to Louis Paulhan as Paulhan prepares to make his first solo flight in the hydroplane. Before Paulhan took off, however, Robinson insisted that "his" number 13 be removed from the radiator.

the beach behind the casino. When assembled, they nested in the hangar like huge ospreys. Robinson coached the well-seasoned Paulhan on flying the hydro, and soon the two men were flying frequent exhibitions (fig. 57). They flew for the public as well as for various governments in their introduction of the Curtiss hydroplane to Europe.

A newspaper report to the *St. Louis Post-Dispatch* on February 8, 1912, stated,

> In the hydroaeroplane tests at Juan-les-Pins this afternoon, the American Aviator, Mr. Robinson, gave an exhibition with a Curtiss machine, rising several times from the water and returning to the water again. The experiments were very successful. Mr. Paulhan was present and followed the exhibition closely, while Commander Coffinieres De Nordeck, representing the French Navy, was also present. Another hydroaeroplane exhibition will be given on Saturday.

A clipping from France reported,

> Antibes, Wednesday: Mr. Robinson today made seven splendid flights with a Curtiss hydroaeroplane at Juan-les-Pins, carrying Captain De Boys, of the French Army, in one flight and Lt. Stachovskis, of the Russian Navy, in another. M. Louis Paulhan made three lengthy flights in the same machine. Mr. Robinson shut off the motor when at an altitude of 600 meters during one flight, alighting alongside the battleship Voltaire as easily as a gull riding the waves. This was a part of the demonstration arranged for the officials present. They were in a motorboat which towed the hydroaeroplane ashore.
>
> During one flight, Mr. Robinson rose to an altitude of 700 meters and attained a speed of ninety-five kilometers an hour.

An account from Nice reported, "General R. has designated Lt. Iocca to follow the lead set by M. Paulhan and take the lessons necessary to become proficient in the handling of the Curtiss hydroaeroplane."

The extensive French naval forces cruising off the coast of southern France gave Robinson, ever the showman, another great promotion idea: why not fly out to Admiral Moreau's ship, the *Justice,* and drop an invitation for a banquet to be held in the casino at Juan-les-Pins the next day? Robinson penned an invitation to the admiral and attached it to an American flag and a bag of sand. After flying over the French fleet, he dipped low, dropping the sand bomb onto the deck of the admiral's flagship. The invitation was picked up from the deck by an officer and handed to the admiral, who remarked that it was the first time he had received an invitation in such a manner.

A magnificent feast was served on February 11 to the admiral and the other dignitaries, and the two aviators attempted to persuade the guest of honor that the hydro was a great device for his fleet. They did not know that Admiral Moreau had already telegraphed the results of the hydro flights to the minister of marines and requested that an officer be assigned to follow up.

On the day of the banquet, the weather was windy and rainy, and

Robinson suffered another lapse in judgment by insisting that the hydro-plane was safe to fly at such times. To prove this, he declared to one and all that he would fly the plane immediately after the banquet. Though a newspaper had previously reported that Robinson would take some of the banquet guests for an airplane ride, all were impressed with Robinson's decision to fly in the wind and rain.

The hydro was readied on the shore, despite the gray skies overhead. Robinson took off into a gust of wind that nearly flipped him over before he could become airborne. The takeoff was successful, however, and Robinson circled over the beach at five hundred feet, having observed that the waves were running much higher than when he had taken off. The flight went well until he reached this altitude, at which point the controls went slack and, with the motor wide open, the plane went into a spin (figs. 58 and 59).

Robinson reported as follows:

> It all happened so suddenly the only thing I could remember to do was to jump just before the plane hit the water a half mile offshore. I landed feet first, the shock stunning me so that it took some seconds before I started feebly to tread water. My clothes had all been forced up under my chin and there I floated, my head and nose burning like fire from salt water forced into me. How long I floated I don't know, but as I was washed ashore by the waves, I heard music and bells. If this was dying, it was rather pleasant, I thought. Then I became very sleepy and was conscious of slipping beneath the surface without making any effort to keep swimming. At that moment, the observers on shore and those wading to meet me said that I leaped into the air spurting water like a harpooned whale. What had happened was I had drifted into rather shal-low water and, as I sank, my feet touched bottom. The shock of feeling something solid under me brought me to my senses and I leaped up to save my life. In a few minutes rescuers had reached me and assisted me to the beach.

Robinson was discouraged and embarrassed by the incident. A reporter on the scene made several sarcastic comments, and Paulhan knocked him

58. What appears to be a small black spot in the water is Robinson at the moment of impact.

59. The twisted wreckage of the hydroplane being pulled from the water after Robinson's spectacular crash into the Mediterranean.

to the ground. Robinson felt he had let Curtiss and his team down. Nevertheless, Admiral Moreau returned several days later to accept the previous invitation to ride with Robinson. The admiral was superstitious and stipulated that he would fly with Robinson only if the number 13 was removed from the radiator. When this was done, the admiral had his ride.

Much to the surprise of Robinson and Paulhan, orders for the hydroplanes came pouring in. Men in aviation worldwide were impressed that a pilot could fall so far in a spin and survive without a scratch. The New York newspapers carried the story, as did the European press. Overall, the incident in which Robinson initially believed he had disappointed Glenn Curtiss proved to be a huge boost for sales and the advancement of hydroplanes generally. Many aviators concluded that pilots could be trained over water more safely than over land, as the pilots could suffer at worst a thorough soaking. This belief saved many lives over the years.

Robinson remained at Juan-les-Pins to prepare for the world's first hydroplane meet, which was to be held at Monte Carlo in March. The contest was to be sponsored by the International Sporting Club of Monaco, a prestigious, somewhat clannish group. Robinson would receive a stipend of fifteen hundred dollars a day to perform in his hydro as one of the features of the meet.

The Curtiss team felt they had a good chance of winning, because they believed the Curtiss hydro could outperform the other planes in every way. Its smaller, lighter size enabled the craft to be maneuvered more easily than the larger European craft. The larger foreign hydro, however, could carry more passengers, and this was an important feature of the exhibi-

60. Robinson and Shack, the latter wearing his usual brimmed hat, on the beach at Monte Carlo in 1912. The Curtiss hydroplane was being prepared for the world's first International Hydroaeroplane Meet. Note Robinson's lucky 13 on the radiator, wings, and tail.

61. Hugh Robinson and his hydro in the harbor at Monte Carlo.

tion. Many of the European aviators also had copied the Curtiss pontoon and affixed it to their hydros, causing the Curtiss group additional concern about their competitors. Robinson and his cohorts felt that, if the other machines should overshadow Curtiss's hydro during the meet, Curtiss would lose valuable contracts to other companies (fig. 60).

The aviation meet started on schedule, even though the first day was calm, making it difficult to take off from the water, especially with heavy loads (fig. 61). Many different events had been planned for each day of the seven-day meet, and at the end of each day the exhibition officials would total the points. The events included contests for fastest takeoff, greatest passenger-carrying capacity, and longest flight. On the final day of the meet, all pilots were required to land on water, beach their hydros, turn their aircraft around, and take off again without getting their feet wet.

Robinson won many of the events, but as he and his teammates had feared, he did not win the passenger-carrying contest. At the last moment—and apparently to give the large French machines an advantage— a new provision was added that would credit pilots with an extra thirty percent of that day's total points for each additional passenger they could

62. *The Henri Farman biplane, piloted by Fischer, won first place. This large hydroplane was capable of carrying several passengers. Note the twin pontoons on this model as opposed to the Curtiss-designed single float.*

carry. As a result, Paulhan and Robinson finished third and fourth respectively. Farman airplanes placed first and second. French pilots Caudron, Sanches-Besa, and Voison placed fifth, sixth, and seventh in the exhibition (fig. 62).

At the close of the exhibition, Robinson gave a special flying display before several crowned heads of Europe. At the conclusion of his performance, he was presented with a pin consisting of an arrangement of diamonds and rubies that formed his insignia, the lucky 13. He was also given a special bronze medal by the International Sporting Club. A banquet was held in his honor at the Monaco casino. Robinson and the prince of Monaco became good friends, and Robinson was given an Egyptian drinking cup from the prince's famous museum at Monte Carlo.

This exhibition marked the end of Hugh Robinson's work in Europe, but he remained several weeks longer to attend a motorboat race. Stormy weather prevented further flying. While crossing the Atlantic after his prolonged stay in Europe, he learned that the ship on which he had originally been scheduled to return home had gone down after hitting an iceberg. It was the SS *Titanic*. Robinson had managed to defy death once again.

CHAPTER 8

Hammondsport,
New York, 1912

By early April 1912, Hugh Robinson had returned to Hammondsport to prepare for the hydro races in New York, the first to be held in this country. At this time Robinson was gratified to learn that orders for the Curtiss hydro had begun to come in from several foreign countries as a result of his demonstrations in Europe. Louis Paulhan ordered two hydros for himself, making plans to manufacture them under a new royalty agreement with Curtiss.

Following the New York races, Robinson returned to aviation engineering and instructing at the Hammondsport Curtiss School of Aviation, where he was the first hydroplane instructor. In the ensuing months as head instructor he taught scores of would-be pilots, both American and foreign, to fly the hydro. Most of his students considered him a nervous teacher because he would not allow them to move their control stick more than an inch before he grabbed the duplicate controls, a device that provided some safety (fig. 63). Another safeguard was teaching students the mechanics of flying on shore before they were allowed to attempt takeoff from the water. Robinson set a world record by making fifty-six flights in one day, each with a different student, with each flight lasting eight to ten minutes, for a total of more than eight hundred miles.

On June 9, Robinson made what was probably the first emergency medical flight, taking Dr. P. L. Alden four miles from Hammondsport to Urbana,

63. An unnamed student holds on to the rope tied around the hem of her dress. Since she would be thus incapacitated in the event of a dunking, she had to wear a life preserver. Robinson's expression here is a bit less stern than usual.

New York, to assist a young boy who had severely broken his leg in a fall (fig. 64). The Hammondsport paper reported the event thusly:

> Sunday afternoon Dr. P. L. Alden received a call to come to Urbana to attend a son of Edward Petrie who had fallen from the first landing of the steps leading to the office of the Urbana Wine Cellars.
>
> The doctor started in his automobile and met Mrs. Hugh Robinson at the Wadsworth House corner, and asked her if she could not ask her husband to take him to Urbana in a hydro-aeroplane to set a boy's leg. No sooner said than done. She had the husband's consent, who told the doctor to meet him at the hangar in five minutes. They met as agreed, had their pictures taken in the hydro, and were off. In eight minutes they landed at Urbana, four miles distant. The boy's thigh bone was set, and the two were back in Hammondsport, the return trip being made in five and a half minutes, alighting on and arising from the water twice.

It was a novel experience, and was probably the first time a physician had ever made a professional call in a hydro-aeroplane or flying machine of any kind.

Dr. Alden describes the sensation as delightful, especially when the hydro was in the air. On the water he says the contact of the pontoons, or boats, with the waves, at a speed of fifty miles an hour is not so pleasant. But the doctor is talking seriously of trading his automobile for a hydro—sometime—maybe.

Although Robinson had given up exhibition flying in the pusher, he performed in the hydro at Bay City and Saginaw, Michigan, in July. Back in Hammondsport, he assisted in the first flight tests of the new Curtiss flying boats. These contained enclosed hulls where the pilot would sit. It had now became apparent to Robinson that his hydro with the lucky 13 on it was fast becoming obsolete.

64. Dr. P. L. Alden, who made the first medical emergency flight. Robinson took him from Hammondsport to Urbana, New York, a distance of four miles, to help a boy with a broken leg.

Robinson performed his last exhibition in the hydro on October 7. He was in Washington, D.C., to install a new type of pontoon on Curtiss's hydroplanes and improve a new system that allowed the pilot to start the engine from his seat. In his flight at the War College, he flew up the Potomac River and circled the Washington Monument—another first, as this had never been done in a hydroplane. Robinson must have decided to go out in style, because a news article described this flight as follows:

> As he raced toward the monument at an altitude of about 1000 feet, Robinson . . . startled the many persons who were looking from the window of the Washington Monument and who were assembled in the White House parking lot, when he suddenly made a sheer drop of more than 400 feet aiming directly for the point which marked the top of the monument. A cry of horror arose from the spectators, but when a few feet from the top of the highshaft, Robinson suddenly swerved and twirled around the monument at a sharp angle.

Shortly after Robinson's trip to Washington, a Neosho newspaper reported his retirement from exhibition flying:

> Mrs. James Robinson received a letter yesterday from her son, Hugh, stating that he had purchased a large amount of stock in the Curtiss Aeroplane Company located at Hammondsport, New York. Hugh now has charge of the experimental work and school of instruction at that place and has given up all flying except trials and Hydro work. He has purchased for himself a motor cycle and also a fine motor boat which he will use on a large lake near Hammondsport. . . .
>
> That Aviator Robinson has given up at least all dangerous flying will be welcome news to Hugh's many friends. Although the fame he has won and the remarkable record he has made have been gratifying to us all, yet the danger attached has always been present, and it is with a feeling of relief that we learn of his entering the safer side of the business.

By this time Robinson had flown approximately six hundred exhibition flights and had accumulated more than two hundred thousand dollars in winnings, a considerable amount of money in 1912. The throngs

65. *The new Curtiss flying boat made the hydroplane obsolete.*

were no longer captivated by the sight of an airplane. Audiences would never be the same as they had been in 1911, when most people, jamming the dusty circus route of daredevil pilots, saw a human being fly for the first time.

After this announcement, Robinson directed his attention to the sleek flying boat that Curtiss was developing (fig. 65). As one of the early boat racers, Robinson had his own ideas about the design of the flying boat. But when his old St. Louis friend Tom Benoist came to Hammondsport to see the Curtiss flying boat, Benoist attempted to lure Robinson away from Curtiss and eventually succeeded. Benoist wanted Robinson to help him design and build his own flying boat. He made Robinson a design engineer, along with him and Tony Jannus. He sold Robinson stock in the company and made arrangements for him to begin work in St. Louis that November.

The Benoist Flying Boat, St. Louis, 1913

Plans for the new Benoist flying boat were developed by Robinson and Tom Benoist. Robinson was now directing its construction, which took place at the St. Louis Trolley Car Company (fig. 66). The craft was a biplane twenty-two feet long with a six-cylinder, seventy-five-horsepower Roberts engine. Unlike the Curtiss flying boat, this one's engine was mounted deep in the surrounding hull and drove the high pusher propeller by a chain drive. The low-mounted engine was an innovation, and Robinson and Benoist's flying boat was the first one in the world designed in this manner. It created a low center of gravity, which gave the airplane more stability at slower speeds. The biplane was designed to carry two passengers or two hundred pounds of freight (fig. 67). Its list price was to be $4,150, including an extra propeller. The two men figured that production would take about two months.

In early January 1913, Robinson and Tony Jannus conducted the first test flights of the latest Benoist design, Model 13, on Creve Coeur Lake (figs. 68 and 69). Later that month the biplane was displayed for a week at the St. Louis Motorboat Show as the latest item every sportsman should have. It combined a maximum of safety, comfort, and speed—all selling points.

After the boat show, all flight tests were postponed because the lake had iced over. By then the flying boat had been properly balanced and the

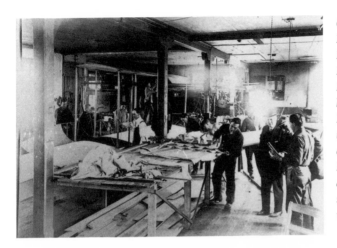

66. Workers in the Benoist Aircraft Factory in St. Louis built the Benoist flying boat, which Robinson helped to design and construct. Robinson is shown at left center supervising the work.

67. Tom Benoist seated behind Hugh Robinson in their new flying boat, which Robinson claimed would replace the older hydroplane that had become obsolete. Behind is the St. Louis Streetcar Company building, which housed the Benoist Aircraft Factory.

*68. Robinson's
Model 13 hull
with a Roberts
two-cycle boat
engine for the
Benoist flying
boat.*

*69. At Creve Coeur Lake the new Model 13 Benoist flying boat was reassembled for testing.
Many test flights and modifications were made before public flights on the craft began on the
Mississippi River.*

70. By March 1913 Robinson was flying above the Mississippi at speeds of eighty-five miles per hour. The airboat, which had a seventy-five-horsepower engine, was nearing commercial usage with safe and powerful flights. The towboat pulled the airboat to and from the river's edge during the flights and also provided a means of rescue in the event of accidents.

flotation mechanism perfected. The new craft was taken to the Mississippi River waterfront in St. Louis for further testing. The plane remained on the riverfront for weeks as the men waited for the cold, snowy weather to clear. Finally, thousands of spectators were treated to a series of spectacular daily flights performed by Robinson and Jannus. A few small changes, mainly cosmetic, were made as the Benoist flying boat was perfected and readied for commercial sale. By March 13 Robinson and Benoist had modified the Model 13 with trailing edge ailerons and renamed it the Lake Cruiser (fig. 70).

Robinson returned from his so-called retirement from exhibition flying, performing in the Benoist plane at Paducah, Kentucky, on May 13. He presented another exhibition at Hannibal, Missouri, shortly afterward. In Duluth, Minnesota, however, while preparing the Benoist flying boat for the Great Lakes Cruise Airshow in Chicago, he experienced a serious crash that wrecked the latest aircraft, the Lark of Duluth (fig. 71), and injured Robinson and his mechanic, Wells Ingalls. Robinson was cut and almost blinded by a snapped brace, while Ingalls was merely bruised. The two

71. *The Lark of Duluth.*

men were saved from drowning by a nearby rescue boat. The Sunday magazine of the *St. Louis Post-Dispatch* reported the accident as follows:

At Duluth, Minn., Robinson was flying over the water in a hydroaeroplane [sic] with a system of controls new to him. His companion was a mechanic, Wells Ingalls, who could not swim. As they alighted on the water at a speed of nearly a mile a minute, the aviator instinctively pulled back the rudder lever, as he was accustomed to do with other machines. However, instead of lessening the shock of landing as he had intended, the lever jerked the horizontal rudder about, and the craft swerved to one side with such violence that its hull and the wings parted company.

Ingalls was flung 15 feet away in the water, and Robinson received a blow on the head from a strut which dazed him. But he saw the mechanic's hair and perceived that, though he was paddling desperately, he could not get his head above water.

The aviator disentangled himself from a network of broken wires and swam to the other's assistance. Ingalls seized him with the grip of the drowning and forced him under water. Robinson, unable to free himself, swam under water at random, and by good luck, at last reached the wings of the biplane which were still floating. Ingalls at once loosed his hold on Robinson's neck to grasp the framework. But as a last annoyance, Robinson's coattails got tangled in the engine under water, and by the time he released himself and reached the surface he was utterly spent.

The boat had been bought by William D. Jones, and now it could not be delivered. This was quite a blow to Benoist and Robinson. The Lark was returned to St. Louis and, during the following months, was rebuilt from what remained of its wreckage.

Benoist decided to move with his rebuilt plane to Tampa, Florida, where he established the world's first commercial airline, the St. Petersburg-Tampa Airboat Line. According to his plan, the company would offer two round-trip flights daily except Sundays between Tampa and St. Petersburg. The twenty-two-mile trip across Tampa Bay would cost five dollars a person one way. Robinson, however, was not with Jannus and Benoist when they traveled to Florida to set up their first venture. Serious differences of opinion had gradually separated him and Benoist, and despite his stock holdings, Robinson left the firm near the end of the year.

The crash of the Lark of Duluth was Robinson's fifteenth narrow escape from death, and he decided that the time really had come for him to stop flying. He had reached a period in life at which he thought he should settle down to a more normal style of living. Toward this end he purchased two movie theaters in St. Louis and proceeded to manage them, but, having become accustomed to the exhilaration of flying, he soon became restless. He was a performer and an inventor as well as an engineer, and he longed for the excitement of his former life. Much to the chagrin of his family, he was soon back in the barn redesigning the Circle of Death, the contraption in which he had done his early circus performances.

Improving upon his earlier Circle of Death, Robinson designed a lattice loop twenty inches wide and fourteen feet in diameter, in which he planned to speed around and around on a motorcycle at forty miles an hour. This would be an exciting advancement over his earlier performance on a bicycle. To achieve this speed, he would use a saucer-shaped platform, upon the curb of which he could go around and around until the wheel of the motorcycle was spinning fast enough to propel him into his loop at the necessary speed. The platform would then be removed, and the entire loop structure would be controlled by an electric motor that would cause it to revolve on its axis. This would allow the rider to be seen from all angles.

The first time Robinson tested his new invention, the motorcycle broke through the loop, and Robinson went flying with it through the side of the barn, somehow sustaining only minor injuries. From this experience he realized that a lighter engine was needed for the motorcycle, and he set about rebuilding his revolving treadway. After refining the design, Robinson started a vaudeville act named the Circle of Death, in which he was the first person to loop-the-loop on a motorcycle. He was described in one advertisement as a human gyroscope. Soon, however, he became weary of performing and trained two other men to do the trick. When one of them was killed in a performance, Robinson dropped the act.

Now missing aviation, Robinson called his old friend Glenn Curtiss and confessed that, for him, retirement was more dangerous than flying. At the age of thirty-two, Robinson went to Buffalo to work as an engineer at the Curtiss Aviation Plant. He worked on the new Jenny design and its OX-5 engine as well as the H-4 flying boat. In January 1914 both were being developed for use in World War I. There was much work to be done with the new tractor-type Jenny, and there were English pilots to be trained. Robinson took part in all phases of this work and made significant contributions to Curtiss's war effort.

The old ways were changing. Mass production methods were required to meet orders totaling millions of dollars, and the aviation pioneers were being put out to pasture by new aeronautical engineers coming out of such institutions as Massachusetts Institute of Technology. The new designers understood drafting and efficient new design methods. No longer were airplane designs drawn to size on a workshop wall to be used as construction guides in building models from wood, fabric, and wire. No longer were the test pilots the same men who had designed and built the airplanes. No longer did a designer-builder-pilot use every means to find a practical application for his creation and then find a market for it. This situation was painful for the earlier engineers, such as Robinson, who were only in their mid-thirties yet already becoming obsolete.

Aeromarine Plane and Motor Company, Keyport, New Jersey, 1917–1924

Hugh Robinson left Curtiss in 1917 for a position as general superintendent at the Aeromarine Plane and Motor Company in Keyport, New Jersey. It was an opportunity for him to do the kind of work he liked the
most, hands-on aircraft development, much as he had done in San Diego
with the hydroplane.

At Keyport he had excellent facilities for his creative endeavors. When
the United States entered World War I in 1917, large sums of money were
appropriated for the manufacture and development of aircraft. Great Brit-
ain also ordered many airplanes, which had to be dependable and able to
fly long distances. Engineers developed new methods to test the capabilities of aircraft from tail to propeller. They learned to determine exactly
how much stress and strain a plane could withstand. Science was taking
over.

While he was in Keyport, Robinson developed the Cootie Model R-13,
a sporty biwing airplane that weighed only six hundred pounds (fig. 72).
It carried two persons, had a thirty-horsepower engine, flew eighty-one
miles per hour, and climbed at a rate of two hundred feet a minute. It was
priced to sell for eighteen hundred dollars. The war put an early end to
sport flying, however, and Robinson's attention returned to military aviation.

72. *The Cootie Model R-13 flew eighty-one miles per hour and was one of the world's first sports planes. Developed at Aeromarine at Keyport, New Jersey, it was test-flown by its inventor, Hugh Robinson, and later crashed on Long Island with no fatalities.*

The New Jersey factory of Aeromarine developed many excellent airplanes during the war and was considered a first-rate operation. It was ideally located next to its own landing strip and water access. Pontoons were put on the land planes, and they were flight-tested on the water, a safer place for testing. Following the end of the war, the firm produced a flying boat that was the mainstay of the company's Florida subsidiary, Aeromarine Airways, in Miami (fig. 73). Planes from this factory flew against the backdrop of the Miami skyline, and the city was just developing its own aviation wings by opening Latin America to future flights between the Americas.

Nine out of ten commercial carriers now used flying boats exclusively

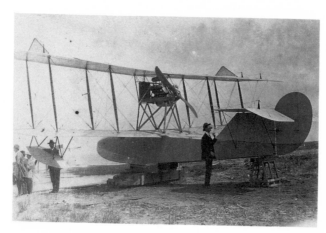

73. The Model-40 flying boat being assembled on the beach. Robinson is shown directing operations at the tail of the aircraft.

on their air routes as transport aviation made its precarious start. The postwar slump was devastating for aviation. There was an enormous surplus of airplanes, and most of the large aircraft companies fell on lackluster times and went bankrupt. By 1924 the Aeromarine Company had produced its last aircraft.

Incidental fame came to Robinson's son Harold, who had never been interested in aviation and had never designed or flown aircraft but was extremely adept at developing radios. Together, Harold and his father built a radio that made its own bit of history on October 6, 1920 (fig. 74). Harold, an amateur disc jockey, played a record on that night that, because of stratospheric conditions, was heard in Aberdeenshire, Scotland. Thus the two Robinsons were credited with the first transmission of the human voice across the Atlantic (fig. 75).

74. *Harold and Hugh Robinson next to the shortwave radio set they put together in New Jersey. On October 6, 1920, the radio transmitted sound to Scotland, thirty-five hundred miles away, as the Robinsons learned from a postcard they received from that country.*

75. *A billboard outside Keyport proclaims the first radio transmission across the ocean.*

CHAPTER 11

Forty More Good Years:
Miami to Maryland, 1924–1963

Glenn Curtiss had accumulated a fortune estimated at thirty-two million dollars when he retired in 1921. At that time he was only forty-one years old, with plenty of energy left to try his hand at ranching and land development in southern Florida. He joined forces with James Bright, the owner of a seventeen-thousand-acre ranch just north of Miami. Anticipating the Florida land boom, the men became business partners and proceeded to purchase the surrounding wilderness for two to three dollars an acre until they owned a massive amount of land. In 1921 they had excavated the Miami Canal for grading and had developed a piece of land that would become part of the original Bright ranch. The lots sold as quickly as they could be sectioned, and the area became the town of Hialeah, where Curtiss built his first home.

Pursuing their dream of building a residential paradise, Curtiss and Bright then developed Country Club Estates, a small town now known as Miami Springs. There Curtiss built his second home in a style similar to that of the pueblos of the Southwest. The partners then decided to expand their development to include the land north of Hialeah and Country Club Estates. This area was named Opa-Locka, and it became the third city developed by the two partners.

When the plans for Opa-Locka were being formulated in 1924, Hugh Robinson contacted Curtiss in search of employment. Robinson had re-

76. Glenn Curtiss came to Florida in 1924 to retire and helped build the Arabian Nights*–inspired town of Opa-Locka just north of Miami. This photo shows the town's city hall.*

cently retired from the Aero-marine Airplane Company and longed for the old days he had enjoyed with Curtiss during the infancy of aviation. Curtiss invited Robinson to help in the development of Opa-Locka. Other friends and employees who had struggled together during the early days had also joined Curtiss in his new venture. Robinson was thrilled to have the opportunity to rekindle the spark of adventure they had known together. He sold his New Jersey home and moved with his family to Opa-Locka, where they were among the first inhabitants.

Curtiss had envisioned Opa-Locka as a special place where people would have enough space to garden and where industry could grow. It was the idea of Bernhardt E. Mueller to build the city on an *Arabian Nights* theme, naming the streets after characters from that series of stories, and Robinson became one of the builders. Opa-Locka's city hall resembled a mosque (fig. 76), and the plan for the city included an archery club, a golf club, riding stables, a zoo, and beautiful gardens along with hotels, banks, stores, and the other necessary components of a city. As a result of its unique architecture and design, around 1926 Opa-Locka became the fashionable place for Miamians and tourists to visit. The Seaboard Airline Railroad made Opa-Locka its first stop out of Miami.

Robinson became a member of the original Opa-Locka town council as well as the city's fire chief (fig. 77). He was an outstanding pioneer citizen of the newly formed community and invested much of his retirement money in it.

The first industry established in Opa-Locka was the Aerocar Company. Here Curtiss and Robinson took the technology they had developed in building airplanes—covering a wooden frame with fabric—and applied it to building custom trailers, which they called aerocars. Curtiss first conceived of the idea because he loved to go hunting in the areas outlying Miami and to go to the beach, but he found transportation and accommodations inadequate and uncomfortable. To meet the need for both, he built a house trailer to be towed by car.

77. The first Opa-Locka town council, seated outside City Hall. In this photo, taken in 1927—three years after the Robinsons had come to Opa-Locka—Robinson is standing in back to the far left. He also served as the town's fire chief.

78. Curtiss's aero-car concept was unique because of the method he designed to provide a smooth ride for both the trailer and the car pulling it. An inflated tire was bolted into a wood frame and attached to the trunk of the automobile, and the trailer hitch was attached to this fifth wheel's axle.

Traveling this way, however, proved to be difficult because of the poor roads; the trailer would jar the automobile and make the ride uncomfortable. To solve this problem, Curtiss developed a trailer hitch that could be attached to the center of a wheel mounted sideways on the trunk of a car (fig. 78). The inflated tire, encased in a firm frame, absorbed most of the bumps and made for a more comfortable ride.

The Aerocar Company of Opa-Locka was housed in a stately *Arabian Nights*–style building. Robinson was in charge of manufacturing and was chief engineer; he later became vice-president of the company. Sayre Wheeler was the company's president (fig. 79).

By 1930 the aerocar had many uses and was a popular seller. Some models were used as passenger cars; others were used as homes and offices and as vehicles for traveling salesmen. The aerocar was expensive; it cost about ten thousand dollars (fig. 80). Gerardo Machado, then president of Cuba, was presented with one as a gift from Carl G. Fisher of Miami Beach and Glenn Curtiss. Philbrick Funeral Home in Miami used the aerocar as a hearse. According to a *Miami Daily News* report on May 25, 1930, "the aerocar afforded speed with comfort and safety, eliminating noise and vibration. The aerocar used aircraft construction which was light and durable."

79. *Robinson during the time he was vice-president, chief engineer, and plant superin-tendent of the new Curtiss Aero-car Company in Opa-Locka, Florida. This photo was taken in the plant where the streamlined trailers were made and hitched to autos for towing.*

80. A 1930s Curtiss aerocar parked in front of the city hall in Opa-Locka.

By 1925 Curtiss had set up two flying fields in the Miami area. One was in Hialeah; the other was on the south tip of Miami Beach. That year Robinson flew a JN-4 "Jenny" out of Hialeah for a short hop—his last flight. Having given some nine hundred exhibitions in the United States and Europe and logged more than three thousand hours in the air, many of them in first flights of new and untried airplanes, he never flew again.

Development in southern Florida suffered a tremendous blow with the 1926 hurricane. Robinson and his family were not gravely affected, however, because the storm's greatest impact was in Miami rather than Opa-Locka. Another factor that had a negative impact on development was the faltering U.S. economy, which was causing a decline in land sales. It was only because of Curtiss's vast fortune that his prospects were able to continue. Curtiss was determined to maintain employment for his loyal friends. On a visit to Buffalo, New York, however, he developed acute appendicitis. Although his appendectomy was successful, soon after surgery, on July 23, 1930, he died from a pulmonary embolism. He was fifty years old.

With Curtiss's death, Robinson lost a close friend and colleague. His fondest memories were of the days he had spent bringing into being the many extraordinary ideas that had sprung from Curtiss's inventive mind, and his companion's passing away left an emptiness in Robinson's life that could not be filled.

Although Robinson was no longer flying planes, his ideas and knowledge were still valued. In 1933 the Aerocar Company moved to Coral Gables. Robinson's son Harold became president of the company, and Robinson continued to supervise construction. By 1939 the plant closed, and Robinson went to work in Deland, Florida, building gliders for use in World War II. After two years he returned to Coral Gables, where he worked as a private consultant to the government and to various aircraft companies.

As part of the war effort Robinson worked from 1940 to 1943 at the Intercontinental Aircraft Corporation in Miami as an engineer, personnel manager, and assistant factory manager. From there he returned to Deland to work for the Babcock Aircraft Corporation as general superintendent for the manufacture of gliders. Late in 1943 he worked as general manager at the Wilson Manufacturing Company in Fort Lauderdale, Florida. This was a revamping factory for new precision war contracts. From there he transferred to the Miami Air Depot, where he worked as director of industrial relations until 1944.

Hugh's son Harold had moved to Maryland, where he established an electronics research lab affiliated with Wedd Laboratories in Washington, D.C. In 1945 Hugh and his wife followed their son to Maryland. There Hugh was hired by Wedd went back to work as a consulting engineer (fig. 82). Here he was awarded a patent on a single-valve system for a small motor he designed.

Now in his sixties, Robinson continued his scientific work, not for money or fame but for the ongoing satisfaction of solving problems. He

81. Robinson, often called the Pioneer Eagle, always dressed for the show, adding style as well as skill to the world of aviation. Pilot 42 was one of a breed of men unique to his times, and he remained his own man to the end.

spent his final working years as a consulting engineer for National Scientific Laboratories in Washington, retiring once more in 1955 at the age of seventy-three. In addition to his other accomplishments, he coedited the *Curtiss Book of Aviation,* acted as technical editor of *Auto Review,* and served as a correspondent for *Aircraft* magazine. On March 26, 1963, he died of a heart attack in his home at Tacoma Park, Maryland.

Unlike most of the daring pilots of the earliest days of aviation, Robinson lived a long, full life. He and his wife raised two sons and were able to enjoy seven grandchildren and seven great-grandchildren. Fortunately, a complete record was kept of Robinson's younger years, when people first dreamed of flying and then lived to see their dreams come true.

Although Robinson had made a comfortable living, he was never a true businessman, rarely submitting patent applications for his various inventions. He did, however, avoid the agony and wasted energy that Curtiss, the Wrights, and other early inventors had to endure in the courts, bat-

82. Even in his later years, Robinson craved the satisfaction of solving problems, so he continued his scientific research. The last position he held was as consulting engineer for the National Scientific Laboratories in Washington, D.C., from 1945 to 1953.

tling over who had invented this and who had patented that. These court battles served mainly to delay the development of aviation, and Robinson had never been attracted to this kind of confrontation.

In many ways Robinson lived at the right time. It was a time of optimism, of new frontiers in communication and transportation. Today the world of aviation is specialized. One can be a mechanic, an aeronautical engineer, a navigator, writer, stunt pilot, or test pilot. Robinson was all of these. Additionally, he taught himself to fly, to repair damaged aircraft, and to create circus acts to promote aviation publicity and raise money to continue his research.

A flying pioneer extraordinaire, Robinson devoted most of his life to early American aviation. He was one of a small group of people who helped Glenn Curtiss establish worldwide recognition in the aircraft industry. Few men did more to assist in the progress of American aviation as it developed into the air transportation we enjoy today.

Although the memory of aviation's pioneers continues to be kept alive by groups interested in historic aviation, the world generally has known little of Hugh Robinson and his remarkable contemporaries. These were the men and women who shared a crystallizing moment in history. We are greatly in their debt.

"A Biographical History of Aviation." In *The Blue Book of Aviation*. Los Angeles: Hoagland, 1932.

Bowers, Peter M. *Curtiss Aircraft, 1907–1927*. London: Putnam's, 1979.

Casey, Louis S. *Curtiss: The Hammondsport Era, 1907–1915*. New York: Crown.

Cleveland, Grover. *Monoplanes and Biplanes: Their Design, Construction, and Operation*. New York: Loening, Munn, 1911.

Curtiss, Glenn H., and Augustus Post. *The Curtiss Aviation Book*. New York: Stokes, 1912.

Fitzgerald-Bush, Frank S. *A Dream of Araby: Glenn Curtiss and the Founding of Opa-Locka*. Opa-Locka, Fla.: South Florida Archaelogical Museum, 1976.

Hatch, Alden. *Glenn Curtiss, Pioneer of Naval Aviation*. New York: Julian Messner, 1942.

Horgan, James J. *The History of Aviation in St. Louis*. Gerald, Mo.: Patrice Press, 1984.

Knott, Richard C. *The American Flying Boat*. Annapolis, Md.: Naval Institute Press, 1979.

Monegasques, Annales. "Revue d'Histoire de Monaco." Monaco: Publication des Archives du Palais Princier, 1981.

Morehouse, Harold E. "Hugh A. Robinson—Early Curtiss Exhibition and Test Pilot—Manufacturing Executive." In *The Flying Pioneers' Biographies*. Washington: Archival Collection of the National Air and Space Museum, Smithsonian Institution.

Provenza, Eugene F., Jr. "Thomas W. Benoist—Early Pioneer St. Louis Aviator (1874–1917)." *Missouri Historical Society Bulletin* (January 1975).

Roseberry, C. R. *Glenn Curtiss: Pioneer of Flight*. Garden City, N.Y.: Doubleday, 1972.

Seely, Lyman J. *Flying Pioneers at Hammondsport, New York*. Auburn, N.Y.: Fenton Press, 1914.

Stark, Jack. "Flying as It Was." *Sportsman Pilot* 24, no. 2 (August 15, 1970): 16–17.

Wright, Wilbur, and Orville Wright. *Heirs of Prometheus*. Edited by Richard P. Hallion. Washington D.C.: National Air and Space Museum, 1978.

Van Deurs, George. *Anchors in the Sky: Spuds Ellyson, the First Naval Aviator*. San Rafael, Calif.: Presidio Press, 1978.

Waterman, Waldo Dean. *Waldo, Pioneer Aviator: A Personal History of American Aviation, 1910–1914*. Carlisle, Mass.: Arsdalen, Bosch, 1988.

White, Gay Blair. *The World's First Airline: The St. Petersburg–Tampa Airboat Line*. St. Petersburg, Fla.: Aero Medical Consultants, 1984.

INDEX

Aero Club of America, 21, 24, 56–57, 67

Aerocar Company, 124–28

Aeromarine Airways, 119

Aeromarine Plane and Motor Company, 118–21, 123

Ailerons, in Robinson's monoplane design, 17

Aircraft magazine, 129

Airmail flights, 88–93

Alden, P. L., 105–7

Arresting-gear system, Robinson's design for, 26, 29

Auto Review, 11–15, 129

Aviation, early developments in, 6–7; Robinson's 1909 article on, 11–15

Babcock Aircraft Corporation, 128

Baldwin, Thomas Scott, 5, 7–8

Ballooning, 5, 7; Robinson's 1909 article on, 11–15

Battleships, aircraft landing on, 26–30

Beachy, Lincoln, xvi, 7, 53, 56–58, 76–77, 79–80, 93

Beck, Paul W., 33–34, 52

"Beer barrel" dolly for hydroplanes, 40–42

Bell, Alexander Graham, 52

Benoist 8 plane, 66

Benoist Aircraft Factory, 111

Benoist, Tom, 19–20, 66, 68, 109–17

Bleriot monoplane, 95

Bright, James, 122

Brookins, Eli, 53

Cairo Citizen, 71

Cairo, Illinois, air show, 70

California Arrow (dirigible), 5

Callan, Lansing, 53

Catapults, as airplane launches, 10, 25

Caudron, 104

Circle of Death, 116

Circle of Death act, 4, 26

Collier, D. C., 24, 39–40

Collier, R. J., 35

Collier's Magazine, 24

Controlled flight, early experiments in, 6

Cooper, John ("Jack") D., 32, 34–35

Cootie Model R-13 airplane, 118–19

Country Club Estates (Miami Springs), 122

Cross-country air races, 79–80

Curtiss Air Exhibition Team, 35, 52–72, 76, 84

Curtiss Aviation Camp, 24, 32–37; military contracts with, 51–52
Curtiss Aviation Plant, 116
Curtiss Aviation School, 52, 105
Curtiss Book of Aviation, 73–75, 129
Curtiss pusher, 20–24, 26–30; development of hydroplane model, 37–44, 50–52, 95; passenger flights on, 48; problems with, 59–62; Rapid City, South Dakota exhibition of, 55–56
Curtiss, Glenn, xvi, xvii, 17–19, 26; Curtiss Aviation Camp and, 32–36; death of, 127–28; dive bombing technique and, 46–47; early passenger flights, 48, 57; Florida development projects of, 122–28; flying boat developed by, 109; Gimbels Brothers Race, 79; hires Robinson, 19; hydroplane developed by, 37–44, 50–52, 73–74, 101–2; Jenny aircraft developed by, 116; on Robinson's skill as pilot, 65

Daily Messenger (Mayfield, Kentucky), 70
Dirigibles, 5, 7–9, 11–15
Dive-bombing technique, Robinson's introduction of, 45–47
Dixon, Cromwell, 7, 53, 84
Dorris Motor Company, 5, 20

Early Bird Aviation Historical Monument, xv-xviii
Earnings for early pilots, 63–64
Edmonton, Canada, Robinson's flight in, 55–56
Ellyson, Ted, 33–35, 48–51
Ely, Eugene, xvi; at Curtiss Aviation Camp, 32; death of, 92–93; at flying exhibitions, 22, 24–30, 36, 58, 78, 80, 89
Emergency medical flight, pioneered by Robinson, 105–7

Fabre, Henri, 39
Fanciulli, Jerome, 53, 62, 86, 96
Fisher, Carl G., 126
Flyer, Robinson's design for, 15–19
Flying boats, 109–17, 119–20

Garros, Roland, 51
Gimbels Brothers Race, 79
Glenn Echo Country Club, 66
Gliders, early experiments with, 7
Godet, Eugene, 53
Gordon Bennett Balloon Trophy, 7–8
Great Aerodome, 6
Great Lakes Cruise Airshow, 113
Griffin, Cagy, 68–69

Hale, W. D., 89
Hallett, George, 33
Hamburg, Germany, Robinson's exhibition flight in, 96–97
Hamilton, Charles, 51, 53, 79
Harkness, Harry, 33–36, 39
Havens, Beckwith, 53, 76
Heneks, Estia Emma (Mrs. Hugh Armstrong Robinson), 5, 34
Henri Farman biplane, 95, 104–5
Hibber, Enid, 68
Hydroplanes: commercial orders for, 101–2, 105; constructed at Curtiss Air Camp, 19, 37–45, 50–52; exhibitions with, 55–56, 73–88; French Riviera flights of, 95–104; improvements to, 73–76; Mississippi River flights of, 88–94; rescues with, 80–82

Ingalls, Wells, 113–15
Intercontinental Aircraft Corporation, 128–29
International Hydroplane Meet, 102–4

International Sporting Club of Monaco, 102, 104

Jannus, Tony, 109–11, 113, 115
"Jenny" aircraft, 116, 127
Johnstone, St. Croix, 80–81
Jones, William D., 115

Kelly, G. E. M., 33–34, 48, 52, 58–59
Knabenshue, Roy, 5, 7

Lake Cruiser flying boat, 113
Lambert, A. B., 66–67
Langley, Samuel Pierpont, 5–6
Lark of Duluth flying boat, 113–15
Longworth, Alice Roosevelt, 57
Los Angeles Times, 45–46

Machado, Gerardo, 126
Mansfield Tribune, 86
Mars, Bud, 53
McCurdy, J. A. D., 53, 56
McHenry, R. C., 53
Merrill, Damon, 32, 34–35, 38, 41
Military planes, first hydraplane as, 51–52
Mississippi River: flying boat tested over, 113; Robinson's flight on, 88–94
Monoplanes, Robinson's early design for, 15–17
Moreau, Admiral, 99–101
Motorcycles, 116

Newsreels, 88
New York Aero Club, 79
New York Herald Tribune, 57
North Island Air Show, 36–37
North Island Camp. *See* Curtiss Aviation Camp
Norton, Charles D., 57

Opa-Locka, Florida, 122–28
Ovington, Earl, 03

Paducah, Kentucky: air exhibition in, 57–58
Paducah New Democrat, 58
Pathé News, 88
Paulhan, Louis, 95–98, 101, 104–5
Pilot's licenses, 56–57, 67–68
Post, Augustus, 53
Propeller design, in Robinson's first monoplane, 18–19

Rarified air phenomenon, 83–84
Ratchet and cable hand pump, 96
Read, Albert C., 86
Red Devil automobile, built by Robinson, 2, 4
Robinson, Harold, 5, 34, 62, 120–21, 128
Robinson, Hugh Armstrong; aviation articles by, 11–15; accidents during flights, 56–66, 71–72, 82–83, 93–94, 100–101, 113–15; at Aeromarine Plane and Motor Company, 118–21; bicycle repair shop of, 2–3; birth of, 2; caution regarding risky flights, 58–65; Circle of Death designed by, 116; Columbia River flight, 82–83; contributions to aviation by, xvi; cross-country races by, 79–80; at Curtiss Aviation Camp, 32–37; Curtiss' hiring of, 19–21; death of, 129; dirigible and ballooning activities of, 5–9; dive-bombing concept of, 45–47; early bicycle experiments of, 1–2; emergency medical flight by, 105–7; exhibition flying by, 52–72, 76–94; family life of, 61–63; first airmail flight of, 88–93; first monoplane design (Flyer), 15–18; flies Curtiss pusher, 21–22, 24–26; Florida development project with Curtiss, 123–

28; flying boats and, 109–17; French Riviera flights, 95–104; hydroplane prototype developed by, 37–44, 50–52; "Jenny" aircraft design and, 116; marries Estia Emma Heneks, 5; Mississippi River flight, 88–94; Model 13 hull design, 112–13; passenger flights by, 48; pilot's license attempted, 56–57; pilot's license received by, 66–68; rescues with hydroplane by, 80–82; retirement of, 107–9, 129–30; San Bernadino air show, 49–50; teaches at Curtiss School of Aviation, 105–6; World War II work of, 128

Robinson, Hugh Jr., 5, 62, 69
Rochester Air Show, 74, 76–77
Rodgers, C. P., 89
Russian Aerial League, 74

St. Henry, R. H. "Bob," 34–35, 53, 56
St. Louis Aero Club, 65, 67
St. Louis Air Show, 65–68
St. Louis Centennial Exposition (1909), 18–19, 89
St. Louis Louisiana Purchase Exposition (1904), 5
St. Louis Motorboat Show, 110
St. Louis Post-Dispatch, 30–31, 98–99, 114–15
St. Louis Trolley Car Company, 110–11
St. Louis World's Fair and Exposition (1911), 88
St. Petersburg-Tampa Airboat Line, 115
San Diego Aero Club, 36–37, 39–40
San Diego Naval Air Station, 52
Schoenberg, L. D., 10
Second International Aviation Meet (1910), 21–22

Shackelford, W. J. ("Shack"), 57, 61, 86–87; at Curtiss Aviation Camp, 32, 34; at exhibition flights, 53–55; French Riviera flights, 96, 102
Shortwave radio, oceanic transmission of, 120–21
Simon, René, 82
Speedboats, Robinson's work on, 9–10
Spreckles Company, 32
SS *Amerika,* 96
SS *Titanic,* 104

Thomas 40 race car, 9–10
Thomas 50 racing car, 9–10
"Tractor" design for hydroplanes, 42–44
Transatlantic flights, 84–86
Triad hydroplane, 43–44
Two-cycle engine, Robinson's patent for, 9–10

USS *Pennsylvania,* 26–30, 42–44

Voison, 104

Walker, John C., 33–34, 48, 52
Walsh, C. F., 53
Walter, Eugene, 53
Ward, James J., 53, 58–59, 64
Water rescues, by planes, 80–81
Wedd Laboratories, 128
Willard, Charles F., 35, 49, 53
Williston Daily News, 84
Wilson Manufacturing Company, 128
Witmer, Charles C., 34–35, 50–51, 53
Wright, Orville, 6–7, 17, 25, 79
Wright, Wilbur, xvi, 6–7, 10, 17, 25

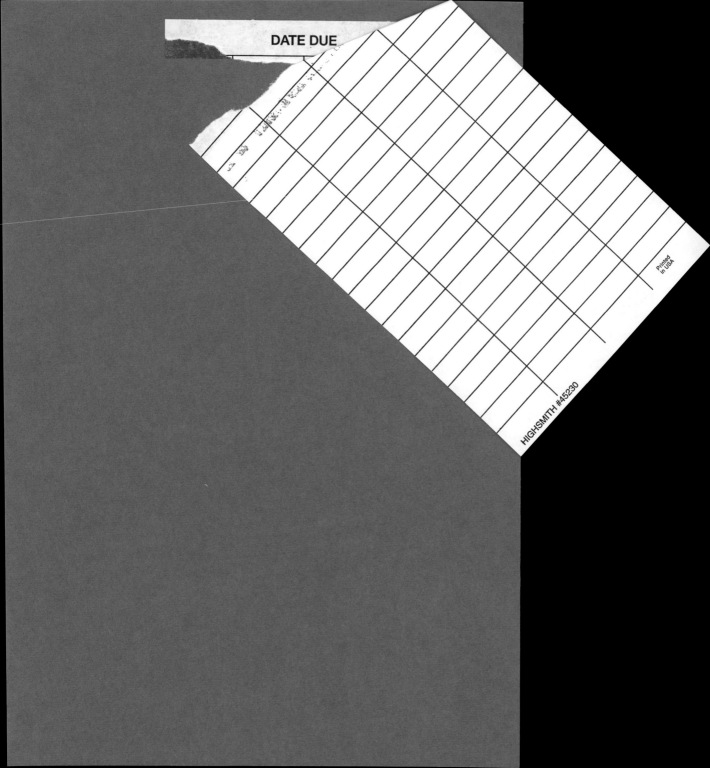